FAITH
THAT TAKES A
LICKIN'

Real People, Real Faith, Real Victories

Jack Coe, Jr.

FAITH THAT TAKES A LICKIN': Real People, Real Faith, Real Victories

ISBN: 0-924748-53-2
UPC: 88571300023-9

Printed in the United States of America
© 2005 by Jack Coe, Jr.

Milestones International Publishers
4410 University Dr., Ste. 113
Huntsville, AL 35816
(256) 536-9402, ext. 234; Fax: (256) 536-4530
www.Milestonesintl.com

1 2 3 4 5 6 7 8 9 10 11 / 10 09 08 07 06 05

Endorsements

Jack Coe, Jr., son of the well-known Jack Coe, Sr., is a wonderful minister of the Gospel, following in his father's footsteps in bringing salvation and healing to many. Jack is a dedicated man of God with a kind and friendly personality, but with a bold faith. He is a man of the Word as well as of the Spirit. I'm sure you will be blessed by the teaching, preaching, and healing ministry of Reverend Jack Coe, Jr.

Jack Coe, Jr., is not only a fellow minister of the Gospel, but also a friend and one whose fellowship I enjoy.

Reverend Ted Rouse
Faith's Creation Christian Fellowship
4400 Mayfair Rd
Milwaukee, WI 53225

At some point in our lives, our faith will be tested. Whether or not we pass the test is solely reliant on our ability to trust and depend on God. *Faith That Takes a Lickin'* is a necessary tool to help people overcome any obstacles they are faced with. Coe's work coupled with the Word of God, not excluding Divine guidance, will ensure that the serious believer will become completely fortified in faith.

Bishop LeRoy Bailey, Jr.

Senior Pastor, The First Cathedral

Author, *A Solid Foundation: Building Your Life From the Ground Up*

Presiding Prelate, Churches Connected and Covered in Covenant

Long before Swatch, Patek-Phillipe's, or Rolex watches became popular in America, I remember enjoying watching Timex watch commercials that boasted its keeping on ticking after all the competitors died off. That very concept has been a valuable lesson in my Christian experience. We are called to last after everyone else has died off. This book is just the guide to show you how to do that. Read it and last.

Aaron D. Lewis

Author, *Keys to Unlocking Your Destiny, Healing for the 21*st *Century*, and *The Total Package: Keys to Acquiring Wealth and Walking in Divine Health*

No matter how hard you try to escape it, nobody on earth will ever be able to really live the life of Christ without having enduring faith. We need all the help that we can get to strengthen our faith. *Faith That Takes a Lickin'* adds to the tall list of necessary aides.

Dr. Kervin J. Smith

Author, *Living Single: The Different Faces of Singlenes*

President, Kervin Smith Ministries

Contents

꿍꿍꿍

Foreword

We are living in times when God is building His church in a way He never did before. God is building a foundation that is marked by strong and solid relationships between churches, leaders, and members, but especially between leaders and pastors. Loyalty and faithfulness are the most important characteristics that hold this foundation together. Without them the apostolic church cannot be built.

God puts certain people together on purpose because He is continuing this work in these times for only one reason: the building of the kingdom, for the Bible says He is coming for a church without spot or wrinkle. We cannot do this by ourselves; we need to trust God to put us together with the people He has chosen to build on and build with.

We are convinced that God has given us this kind of relationship with Jack. And we see this kind of divine relationship very clearly when we are with Jack, his family, and his church. The prophetic words he has spoken over our work, church, and people have all came to pass very precisely and fast. Through this God-given relationship, God has poured out a new growth in our church, especially in the financial area. We consider Jack and his family to be very close friends who are very dear to us, and we thank God for this special and divine relationship!

We believe that as you read this book with faith, it will come alive and God will touch your body and release His blessings into your life.

Dr. Terry and Sylvia Jones
Christliche Gemeinde Köln
Bremerhavenerstr. 23
50735 Köln   Germany

Introduction

It always amazes me, as I travel throughout the world, to discover just how many people have survived major attacks from the enemy. To hear that someone has survived first-degree burns from a fire, the death of their young child or a loved one, an unwarranted divorce, or a long and tiring battle with cancer always gives me a profound sense of respect for the person's dauntless courage. Such courage is the quality we need in order to sustain us when we cannot find support from any other source.

Where do we get that courage? Faith in God is the underlying element that gives us courage in the most hopeless situations and in the face of the most tragic circumstances. There is something uniquely different about the person who chooses to live the life of faith. The faith person never seems to be able to fit in the crowd. One reason such a person cannot fit in is because this type of individual proudly displays and bears the obvious scars of a winner, a victor.

No matter how difficult life seems to get, faith-filled people are always optimistic about the next challenge that is presented, regardless of how hard it may look. They don't try to avoid the test and trial as much as they go through them knowing that, at the test's end, they will receive God's approval, reward, and favor. They know without a doubt that their faith will produce something great within themselves that can be attained only by going *through* the fires of life in faith.

> *My brethren, count it all joy when you fall into various trials, knowing that the testing of your faith produces patience. But let patience have its perfect work, that you may be perfect and complete, lacking nothing* (James 1:2-4).

Contrary to what some may believe, your faith *will* stand trial. It must be tested. Such tests and trials never come to prove to God that you are able to withstand them. God already knows exactly whether or not you will pass the test. God, in His matchless wisdom, also knows exactly when you will pass your test of faith. No, the testing comes to prove to *you* that God has given you all that is needed to win in life.

At times it may appear that your tests will never end. This is not true. The devil will try to convince you that you will always have to go through the same trials. He does this only to discourage you. Don't fall for his lie. Every test has its season. And like the four seasons of winter, spring, summer, and fall, each one eventually comes to an end. However, sometimes one test follows another with such a rapid pace that it seems like you haven't had time to recover from the effects of the previous one. That is just the nature of the faith lifestyle and is par for the course for the person who chooses such a path.

Even though the faith person deals with constant opposition, he or she overcomes every time through the Word of God. Many applaud this characteristic of faith; however, this persistent nature should typify every individual who is a genuine follower of Christ. Every believer must fight to win and then win to fight again. Our aim is to overcome *every* obstacle that the enemy places before us.

And they overcame him by the blood of the Lamb and by the word of their testimony, and they did not love their lives to the death (Revelation 12:11).

What automatically comes to your mind when you hear the witty phrase, "Takes a lickin' and keeps on tickin'!" If you live on the North American continent, it is more than likely that you'll think about watches, particularly Timex watches. For more than 35 years the Timex Corporation has successfully used this motto to reflect the value, durability, and long-lasting quality of their watches.

In fact, this little saying has become such a winning success that it has made Timex watches the most popular and recognized watch brand in North American history, not to mention one of the favorite watches of the world.

In the same way, you can become a favored child of God when you use your faith to conquer life's most trying circumstances. Hebrews 11:6 says, *"But without faith it is impossible to please Him, for he who comes to God must believe that He is, and that He is a rewarder of those who diligently seek Him."* If it is impossible to please God without faith, then by using your faith it is very likely that you will bring pleasure to God. In fact, nothing brings greater pleasure to God than for one of His children to exercise his or her faith.

Unfortunately, too many believers live lifestyles of constant defeat. And such defeat automatically attracts more attack. Think about it. Have you ever seen a vicious dog go after its prey? In most cases the dog will attack more ferociously the person who appears to be in fear. Fear attracts attack, and fear precedes all defeat. Ultimately fear is from the devil, and when we walk in fear we literally partner with the devil.

In this book I will teach you not only what faith is, but also how to use it to conquer the enemy not just once in a while, but *all the time*. I'll share with you the "faith tools" I implemented in overcoming some of the most personally challenging situations I've ever faced in my life. Like

Timex watches, your faith will take a lickin'. However, I am convinced that when you properly understand faith and apply what you have learned, you, too, will be able to last for many decades, still tickin' and standing strong.

Chapter One

What Is Faith?

*F*aith is one of those words that are heard and used often. Not only do Christians of all persuasions use it, but people who do not have a personal relationship with Jesus Christ also use it freely. No matter what religious sect one belongs to, people just seem to use *faith* as the new buzzword in popular culture to identify them as some kind of mystical being.

Overall the word has become misused and improperly applied. As a result, with the widespread misuse of the word *faith*, many Spirit-filled Christians have shied away from pursuing a lifestyle of faith. However, the real reason so many Christians have not pursued faith with diligence is they do not know what faith is from what it isn't. As I travel around the world conducting Healing Explosions, I am often amazed at the lack of knowledge most Christians have about the subject of faith.

I'll often ask a crowd this question: "How many of you know what faith is?" The bewildered looks on most of their faces immediately gives away the truth that they just don't know the answer. They think they know, but they do not. Because they are familiar with the word they may take a stab at answering the question. Most often, they answer incorrectly. What they think faith is, is just not it at all. We will take a look at what faith really is. In order to do that accurately, let's explore what faith is *not*.

Faith Is *Not* a Religion

Millions of people generally think that faith is a religion or a religious organization of some type. Author and church historian Frank Mead, along with Samuel Hill, published a work entitled *Handbook of Denominations in the United States, 11th edition*. In this classic work he lists more than 200 religious groups within the United States. The book deals with the background, doctrinal teachings, and governmental structure of each group.

Mead lists denominations that include not only Christian organizations but also Islamic orders, Baha'i faith, Hindu Communities, Jehovah's Witnesses, and Spiritualist Alliances. Many people believe, when someone mentions "faith," that membership with one of these organizations validates their faith. Have you ever been asked, "What faith are you?" Many people may answer, "Well, I'm a Baptist, a Pentecostal, a Methodist, an Anglican, a Lutheran, or a

Catholic." However, regardless which of these groups you may or may not belong to, your particular choice in church affiliation has nothing to do with what faith really is.

You can be a member of the "Greater First Sanctified Holy Redeemer Church of the Deep Christian Immersion, Inc., Intl.," but that does not mean you have faith. It just means that you have a church to attend. Faith is neither a church nor a denomination. If it were, then you would have to join a particular church or denomination in order to have faith. Faith

Your particular choice in church affiliation has nothing to with what faith really is.

cannot be contained within the four walls of a church or any other structure. Faith is bigger than all that.

Please do not misunderstand what I am saying. In no way am I trying to diminish the value and importance of the local church. I strongly believe in the local church and, because of that, support it with my tithes and offering, my talents and time. Without the continued ministry that the local church provides, our world would be in a most miserable state—far worse off than we are now.

What I *am* saying is that just because you join a particular church, denomination, or fellowship does not automatically qualify you as having faith. Having faith and being a person who walks by faith has far more to do with who you are and what you believe about who

God is. It has to do with His capacity to keep His Word—His ability to never fail, no matter what.

Faith Is *Not* a Feeling—It's a Choice

Another misconception about faith is the one that says faith is a feeling. Faith is not merely a feeling. When you are standing in faith for something, you may feel very strongly that what you are believing for will come to pass. That is perfectly all right. However, you must realize that you do not have to have any feeling or emotion within you in order to release your faith and get results.

There were several times when I believed God for something to come to pass in my life, and I had never felt so spiritually dry in my life. Yet, what I desired came to be. During the least likely time for me to receive what I was expecting, I received it. Other times when I was so emotionally charged and knew that I would have my desire, it failed to come to fruition. Why? The answer is that faith does not require my emotions in order to get a job accomplished.

What exactly is an emotion? An emotion is an affective state of consciousness in which feelings of joy, sorrow, fear, hate, and love are experienced. Another thing that you need to know about emotions is that they waver back and forth much like the waves of the sea. They are never concrete. Emotions change just like a Texas weather forecast. I should know; I'm a native Texan. In one sense emotions are undependable. In another sense they are very unpredictable.

4

You may have a joyful emotion right now, but when circumstances change, your emotions seem to change with them. You'll go from being joyful to sad, happy to mad, hateful to passionate, and so on. If faith was an emotion or even depended on your emotions, you'd be a total mess. The apostle James in his epistle addresses this issue of the instability of our emotions as it relates to faith.

> *If any of you lacks wisdom, let him ask of God, who gives to all liberally and without reproach, and it will be given to him. But let him ask in faith, with no doubting, for he who doubts is like a wave of the sea driven and tossed by the wind. For let not that man suppose that he will receive anything from the Lord; he is a double-minded man, unstable in all his ways* (James 1:5-8).

Faith requires your choosing or, in other words, your will. Although emotional feelings may be present when you begin to do something by faith, they are not necessary. Understand that we are emotional beings. So there is nothing at all wrong with having emotions or being emotional. Just don't allow your emotions to be the basis of your faith or dictate your faith. Your faith should always be dictated or determined by what God's Word says. Thus faith requires your will. You must *choose* to have faith.

No matter how much you want someone else to have faith, it will not happen for him or her just because you want it. You might be very sincere in your desire for another person to experience the faith that you live by and enjoy. As sincere as that desire might be, every individual must have faith for his or her own self. God has given every person an allowance called faith. I personally believe that each of us has been given the same amount of faith at the start of life.

Faith requires an act of your will, not your feelings.

For I say, through the grace given to me, to everyone who is among you, not to think of himself more highly than he ought to think, but to think soberly, **as God has dealt to each one a measure of faith** (Romans 12:3, emphasis added).

The thing that determines how much faith we will have as life goes on is how much we use the faith we now have. If we do not exercise our faith, then we will never increase in faith. The central theme here is that faith is resident in our will. There is not an outside force that can act upon us to cause faith to come. We must consciously will to have faith and act in faith based on the words that we allow to come into our hearing. Faith is a choice.

Faith Is *Not* Based on Senses

We all have been well equipped with natural senses. These senses are any of the functions such as sight, hearing, smell, taste, or touch, by which humans or animals perceive stimuli originating outside or within the body. Faith is neither dependent upon nor limited by that which you can sense: what you can see, what you can hear, or what you can physically touch. Faith is always spiritual. Your senses, on the other hand, can be limited, and they usually are limited by the natural abilities we posses.

Many people believe that if you can see it, then it's real. Faith says just the opposite. If you can't see it, then it's real. Faith gives visible form to that which is not yet seen. Faith is always based on what God's Word declares. Despite what popular opinion believes about reality, God Himself defines what reality actually is through His Word. And there is nothing more real than that which is produced by faith in God's Word's.

Even though people may say, "I'll believe it when I see it," this famous saying actually opposes God's Word, which says something totally different. *"For we walk by faith, not by sight"* (2 Corinthians 5:7). This verse cautions us that in order to walk by faith, we must suspend our sight so that faith may work properly. The more we choose to operate by that which we can see, the less we will experience God's provision in our life.

In 2 Corinthians 4:18 it states, *"While we do not look at the things which are seen, but at the things which are not seen. For the things which are seen are temporary, but the things which are not seen are eternal."* Deeply rooted within this verse is the concept of faith having divinely eternal benefit, while looking to the things that we can visibly see has only temporary value. Your sight can only give you a short-lived blessing. On the other hand, your faith will produce a perpetual supply in your life.

Faith gives visible form to that which is not yet seen. Some people believe that what you touch has a greater quality of realness since it is tangible. The real truth is that the things you cannot touch give credence to faith. It is what makes faith a reality. And, none of those things are based on what we can tap into with our senses. In one sense genuine faith must be totally blind. God speaks it. You obey. It's as simple as that!

You will not always have time to think it over. Time is crucial, so you may not be able to talk this over with your friends and relatives to get their "approval." Most of the time you are just going to have to take action. You are not going to take action because it feels right or because you already know what is going to happen. You do it because you know that obeying God yields great rewards. That's the only basis you need.

Faith Is a Law

Like the law of gravity, faith also works as a law. It is a law set in motion by the greatest authority in the universe, God Himself. This law cannot be revoked; nor can it ever be removed. Once the law of faith has been set in motion, it will continue to produce the desired results as long as it is being acted upon.

The law of gravity simply suggests that whatever goes up must come back down. Gravity is the force set in motion that causes things, when thrust upward, to come down again. It is a natural law. Well, faith is a spiritual law. Much like gravity, faith will work every time. The law of faith says that if you confess and believe that you have received whatever thing you desire, then you will have whatever you say. The Bible gives a scriptural definitive of this law in Mark 11:23.

> *For assuredly, I say to you, whoever says to this mountain, "Be removed and be cast into the sea," and does not doubt in his heart, but believes that those things he says will be done, he will have whatever he says.*

This is a spiritual law already set in motion. If you believe, then you shall receive. Your circumstance, condition, or situation really does not matter. Those things all represent various forms of mountains that are present in people's lives. The mountain could be anything. It could be sickness, disease, financial distress, disharmony in your family, an imminent divorce, possessing the spirits of guilt and shame, or living a lifestyle of perpetual defeat. Whatever your case may be, if you tell (continually confess) your mountain that it has to be removed forever and you refuse to doubt that it will happen, you will have whatever you say.

As with any law, if the law is broken or perverted it will fail to work as intended. This is no different with the law of faith. It, like any other law, must be kept and enforced in order for you to receive its maximum benefit.

Like gravity, the law of faith will work every time.

Money is the currency of earth. Most things that are purchased in the earth realm will be purchased with money. Heaven, on the other hand, operates on a totally different currency—and it's called faith. Operating by the laws of faith is how the believer gets things done in the earth realm. It's our ticket to the supernatural. It is also our guarantee to receiving God's provision for our lives. Faith is the thing that makes heaven respond. When heaven responds, the entire earth has to follow suit. Begin to tap into the law of faith now—believe it and speak it!

And I will give you the keys of the kingdom of heaven, and whatever you bind on earth will be bound in heaven, and whatever you loose on earth will be loosed in heaven (Matthew 16:19).

Faith Is Believing God

If I had to sum up faith in one phrase, it would be this one: Faith is believing God. It's as simple as that. The heart of true faith is believing every word that God says. I realize that for some people this may be tough to accept, tough to digest. God says quite a few things. After all, He has an entire book full of words and promises and predictions.

Is it really possible that everything He says is actually true? Our carnal minds are always at odds with God and His Word. Our carnal nature tries to force a holy God to fit in our agenda. We try to put God in our box. We try so hard to get God to think like us. At the same time, He is offering us the privilege of thinking like Him. But the carnal mind gets in the way and then ultimately stops up the flow of faith that produces results.

> *Because the carnal mind is enmity against God; for it is not subject to the law of God, nor indeed can be. So then, those who are in the flesh cannot please God* (Romans 8:7-8).

> *But without faith it is impossible to please Him, for he who comes to God must believe that He is, and that He is a rewarder of those who diligently seek Him* (Hebrews 11:6).

It is interesting to note that it is impossible for the carnal or flesh-ruled mind to please God, according to Romans 8:7-8. Just as interesting, in Hebrews 11:6, is that it is impossible to please God without faith. What a stark contrast—one that is worthy of deeper probing. On one side, God says that you will displease Him if you have a mind that is worldly. On the other side, you will please God if you operate in faith.

The heart of true faith is believing every word that God says. The thing that causes me to ponder these verses is the fact that they contradict much of our conventional teaching on what pleases and displeases God. In most Christian circles, they will give you a long list of the things that displease the Father. Very seldom will you ever find on their list that the absence of faith in the life of a believer brings God ultimate displeasure.

Now I realize that sin displeases God. And most Christians will draft a list a mile long of all the sins that displease God. They'll tell you that you cannot commit adultery, steal, kill, cheat, lie, lust, and so forth and so on. When I grew up in the Pentecostal church, they would add to the already long list about a thousand or more additional sins that we were to avoid if we were going to live lifestyles that were pleasing to God.

We were told not to go to the movies. We couldn't attend our high school prom. It was a sin to play checkers, marbles, cards, or dominoes because they reflected the nature of those sinful gamblers. Women were forbidden to wear pants or cosmetics. In some circles women were told that it was a sin to wear any type of jewelry. They thought then that making a woman look really good would cause men to lust after her. They forbade wearing perfume because good-smelling scents were too alluring.

Some were forbidden to watch television at all. All of these so-called sins and actual sins were being avoided at all costs in the hopes that these people would bring pleasure to God. Unfortunately, what all of it amounted to was a legalistic church where God never showed up. The glory of God had been replaced by form and ritual. Relationship with the Father had been replaced with trying hard to obey the rules that man had established. Can you see what's wrong with this picture?

The problem is that everyone is doing everything other than what God said to do in order to please Him. "Well, Brother Coe, are you saying that we should just go out and consciously sin because it does not matter?" That's not what I am saying at all. What I am trying to get across to you is that *faith* is what pleases God; nothing more and nothing less. "Then what place does that put the sin issue in?" It puts sin in its rightful place.

Let me explain. The works of the flesh cannot conquer even one of the actual sins mentioned above. Sanctification and holiness are what keep us in a conquering position of victory. However, both sanctification and holiness are produced by faith. That is why it is impossible to please God without faith. Everything from salvation to sanctification to baptism in the Holy Spirit to divine healing is all produced by faith. Without faith none of these things could ever come to pass. Being born again and receiving the salvation of the Lord can never happen without your operating in faith.

Everything in the kingdom of God operates by the law of faith.

But what does it say? "The word is near you, in your mouth and in your heart" (that is, the word of faith which we preach): that if you confess with your mouth the Lord Jesus and believe in your heart that God has raised Him from the dead, you will be saved. For with the heart one believes unto righteousness, and with the mouth confession is made unto salvation. For the Scripture says, "Whoever believes on Him will not be put to shame" (Romans 10:8-11).

Everything in the kingdom of God operates by this law of faith. The only ones who will please God are those who choose to walk by faith. And this walk of faith begins with believing God. If God says that He will supply all your needs, yet you feel that you must help Him do it, then you don't really believe God.

If God told you to leave your job and start the business that you have been dreaming about for years, promising that He would prosper the business, would you do it? Perhaps you would have to give it some deep thought.

Maybe you would have to talk it over with your loved ones. If you wouldn't do it immediately, it is because you don't believe God. That may sound a little hard, but it's true.

If you don't believe Him, then you make Him out to be a liar. Believe me when I tell you that that is not a good thing to call God. If you don't believe God, you will never trust Him. If you don't trust Him, you will never seek after Him. If you never find Him, you'll never be rewarded. Start your faith journey by believing God now!

But without faith it is impossible to please Him, for he who comes to God must believe that He is, and that He is a rewarder of those who diligently seek Him (Hebrews 11:6).

Faith Is an Action Word

There is no faith without action. In other words, you cannot have genuine faith and expect to do absolutely nothing. You will have to show some kind of an action to validate your faith. If you have faith that God will cause financial increase to come into your life, you just can't sit around doing nothing and just expect the money to fall out of the sky. If does not work that way.

You must first sow a financial seed. Your sowing the seed represents the action needed in order for your faith to be properly activated. If you do nothing you will inevitably receive nothing. No matter what area you

15

desire to have biblical faith in, you will have to show action. It is not a matter of trying to help God out. No, He does not need your help. Your action is a reflection of your faith working. In other words, your action makes your faith come alive. Without it your faith will lie in a dormant state.

> *For as the body without the spirit is dead, so faith without works is dead also* (James 2:26).

There are some churches that have faith that their churches will grow larger in membership. Yet they don't seem to be doing any actions to activate their faith. They come to prayer meeting and pray that God will send people into the church. They cry, "Lord, send them in. Send in those wandering lost souls, please, God." They get up from their knees hoping to see every pew filled with hungry souls. To their total surprise, the church is just as empty as it was before they started begging God.

Your action makes your faith come alive.

There is a time to pray and there is a time to act. If you are believing God to send more people to the church, then you must go and get them. People will not come into your church just because they have nothing else to do. You must ask God for wisdom as you create compelling conversation that will cause people to come to Jesus first, then to church.

16

Go put flyers on doors. Personally make it your goal to invite a certain number of people to your church each week. Host an outdoor crusade meeting. Conduct regular street meetings during the warm months. The point is that when you act, when you actually do something, then God will cause your faith to produce results. But it will never happen until you first act on His Word.

> *Then the master said to the servant, "Go out into the highways and hedges, and compel them to come in, that my house may be filled"* (Luke 14:23).

In every area you must show some action, and that action combined with your faith will produce what you believe God to do. Do you know the story of the hemorrhaging woman in the Bible? She had spent all the money she had on doctors in the hope that she would find a cure. Unfortunately, her physicians were not able to cure her. Somehow she heard about Jesus and His awesome power to heal all who were sick and oppressed by the devil. Her story is recorded in the gospels of Matthew, Mark, and Luke.

> *And a woman was there who had been subject to bleeding for twelve years. She had suffered a great deal under the care of many doctors and had spent all she had, yet Instead of getting better she grew worse. When she heard about Jesus, she came up behind him in the crowd and touched*

his cloak, because she thought, "If I just touch his clothes, I will be healed." Immediately her bleeding stopped and she felt in her body that she was freed from her suffering (Mark 5:25-29 NIV).

This woman had faith to believe that she would be healed. She had heard that there was unusual power in the name and in the touch of Jesus. She had one problem. This woman realized that, because of her continual bleeding, she was ceremonially unclean and, therefore, forbidden to be in the company of the common citizens of the community. If she were caught trying to press her way to Jesus or mingling with the crowd, she may have been executed.

Here is a classic example of faith in action. Not caring about the consequences, she took her chances. Perhaps she thought that death would be better than living under the circumstances that were forced upon her. So she acted. She came behind Jesus in the crowd and touched His garment. Immediately she was made well.

What exactly healed this woman? According to the Word, her *faith in action* caused the anointing for healing to flow into her physical body. Had she stood on the sidelines wondering whether or not she should take the chance, she would have died. But she chose to take a major risk—the risk of faith, that is. By doing that she tapped into blessings that were beyond her wildest dreams. The same will happen for you when you put action to your faith.

> *Thus also faith by itself, if it does not have works, is dead. But someone will say, "You have faith, and I have works." Show me your faith without your works, and I will show you my faith by my works* (James 2:17-18).

Chapter Two

Believing Is Seeing

A Faithless Generation

Then Jesus answered and said, "O faithless and perverse generation, how long shall I be with you? How long shall I bear with you? Bring him here to Me" (Matthew 17:17).

Face the truth. For the most part we live in a skeptical and faithless society. For many people, believing something that was written, such as God's Word, or believing something that is heard, such as God's voice, has become a thing of the past. This faithless generation that we live among demands physical proof for practically everything. This craze has gotten totally out of control.

It is so out of control that it is often difficult to determine who are actually believers from who are nonbelievers. Unfortunately, believers are now demanding the same type of proof to explain how and why God does what He does. One thing that we must continue to focus on is the truth that God's actions and thoughts are different than the thoughts of carnally minded people. In fact, they are just the opposite.

> *"For My thoughts are not your thoughts, nor are your ways My ways," says the LORD. "For as the heavens are higher than the earth, so are My ways higher than your ways, and My thoughts than your thoughts"* (Isaiah 55:8-9).

How can you really explain a woman or man who was diagnosed by a physician with a terminal form of cancer, yet who is suddenly and miraculously healed by the power of God? You can't. Medical science and science itself are primarily based on hypothesis, intense research, and experimentation. The majority of the time, if medical practitioners and scientists do not understand how something miraculously happened, they either write it off or they will do further research until they reach a tangible answer—something they can see.

The problem is that most of the things God works in are unseen. He stays in those unseen zones primarily so that humankind can never trace how He does what He does. He stays in the unseen zones to make His God status more clear to the unbeliever. If someone was given three months to live, yet miraculously was healed by the power of Jesus, only the rich in faith can appreciate and accept the healing as a gift, not requiring any further documentation or proof. The believer accepts it as just an act of God's goodness and grace.

God works in the unseen.

The entire goal for the Christian believer should be to think like God thinks and behave as God behaves. The closer we come to His thoughts and actions, the closer we will be to the center of His will and purpose for our existence. If you are a Christian believer, you are not exempt from God's mandate for you to walk by faith. It is your basic duty, not only to please God, but also to live a lifestyle of fulfillment and prosperity. In order to do that you'll have to look at things that you cannot see.

Although the world believes it when they see it, the believer can't afford to wait that long. You have to believe it *before* you see it. More than that, you have to see it once God says it. When you live this kind of faith life, you can always count on having two things. The first thing that you will always have is God's favor and blessing upon your life. That alone is worth the walk.

However, the second thing that is equally as sure is the criticism and ridicule of man. There has never been a person who has truly walked by faith yet been guarded from the criticism of man. It is just a part of the journey. The sooner you accept the fact that you will be ridiculed and talked against, the sooner you will be able to walk with

Jesus on the waters of life. But the key is always keeping your focus on the things that only you and God can visualize.

Looking at What You Cannot See

For we walk by faith, not by sight (2 Corinthians 5:7).

By faith Abraham obeyed when he was called to go out to the place which he would receive as an inheritance. And **he went out, not knowing where he was going.** *By faith he dwelt in the land of promise as in a foreign country, dwelling in tents with Isaac and Jacob, the heirs with him of the same promise; for he waited for the city which has foundations, whose builder and maker is God* (Hebrews 11:8-10, emphasis added).

When I read about the life of Abraham, I am always astounded by his faith in spite of his circumstances. When most men are at the age when they consider retirement, Abraham chooses instead to believe the promises of God. To attain these promises, Abraham would have to leave the place of his origin and his kinsfolk. He also would have to go—by faith—to a place that he has never been before, a place he has not seen.

Now the LORD had said to Abram: "Get out of your country, from your family and from your father's house, to a land that I will show you. I will make you a great nation; I will bless you and make your name great; and you shall be a blessing. I will bless those who bless you, and I will curse him who curses you; and in you all the families of the earth shall be blessed." So Abram departed as the LORD had spoken to him, and Lot went with him. And Abram was seventy-five years old when he depart-ed from Haran (Genesis 12:1-4).

Could you willingly obey God by going somewhere that you have never been? Or do you need a full-color brochure telling you exactly what to expect once you have arrived? People of faith live by a totally different code. We live each day accepting the fact that God may interrupt our plans in order to establish His greater purpose. In doing that, peo-ple of faith are often accused of being a little strange because we get unusually excited over God's promises. And according to other people's viewpoints, those promis-es appear to be an intangible reality.

If you are a person of faith, then you do not have a problem understanding our excitement. On the other hand, if you are a person who is carnally minded, then you will look at the faith person as someone who is imbal-anced and unnecessarily hysterical. We, the rich in faith, get excited about those things that we cannot see. We get all worked up over God's promises. If God says it, then that's it. We believe it and act as if it is already so.

Unlike the promises of man, God's promises are sure. Whatever He says will be, will come to pass. So although others may not be able to see the manifestation of God's promises, faith people see those promises clearly. After all, if you could see it, touch it, and feel it, then you would have no need for faith. The need for faith only applies to the things that you cannot see.

We faith people get excited about things we cannot see.

For example, you may have a serious financial need. In the natural there is no way that you can possibly make ends meet. Added to that, you just discovered that you are going to be permanently laid off from your job this coming Friday. You were already at a financial disadvantage before you found out that you were going to be laid off. The layoff only worsens your situation. On top of all that, you have to meet your monthly expenses that include utilities, your car payment, your mortgage note, and five credit cards.

Those expenses alone total more than $6,000 each month. You have not even included your grocery and automobile gas expenses. Right now all you have to your name is $2,700. It's obvious that you are going to need a financial miracle to meet your need. But wait, I'm not finished yet. God then speaks to your heart and tells you to sow $1,400 (more than half of the money you have) into your ministry. Now you have less money than you started out with, and you need all of it and then some.

You couldn't see your way out before He asked you to give this amount of money to the church. You couldn't see a way out when you discovered that your position was terminated forever. Even if you had been able to keep your job, you still would be in desperate need of a financial miracle because you just do not have enough to break even.

Then God suddenly speaks to your heart, telling you that you are going to receive a $23,000 financial breakthrough—enough to satisfy your debts and have money left over to save and sow. God's speaking to your heart represents *what you cannot see*. That is what you have to keep looking at, as opposed to your need. Look at your provision and the One who is providing for you.

In the natural you can't see it. You don't personally know anyone who could afford to give you that kind of money. Yet, deep down within, you start getting excited at what you can't see. You start embracing the reality of having your debts satisfied and having enough remaining to provide the needed cushion to be able to confidently move forward. Although in the natural you still owe a lot of money, you begin to act like your debts are paid. The once depressive attitude that you wore as clothing has suddenly disappeared because you *know* that you are going to receive a financial breakthrough beyond your thoughts and sight.

The money hasn't arrived yet. Your bills are not paid yet. But, you have actually started looking to purchase things that you have been in need of for some time, even though the physical money is not in your hands. In fact, at your church you make a vow to pay $3,000 toward the purchase of the church's new property.

You made this promise because God told you that money was on the way. That is what you choose to see. Because of that, you have a sense of assurance that everything is fine. You don't have the blues anymore. No, you haven't received the money. However, you have received a promise—and that promise from the Lord is all that you will ever need.

Faith People—A Strange Breed

Faith people are very different than the rest of the people in the world. We see everything a bit differently than others do. We can look at raw undeveloped land with seemingly little potential and see it as the world headquarters for a thriving ministry complete with an administration building, an 800-seat prayer chapel, a state-of-the-art fitness and holistic health center, and an accredited school of world evangelism. The unbelieving owner of the land can't see that deeply.

He saw the land for what it was. It was given to him as an inheritance from his deceased grandfather. Although he wanted to keep the land in the family for several generations, he knew that, with the decreasing property values in the current market, eventually this deeply rural parcel would wind up not being worth anything. So before its value diminished to zero and he ended up without any inheritance at all, he decided to offer the property to a faith person who had big dreams for it. One person couldn't see the value, but the person of faith saw clearly what the owner could not see.

What other people would throw away, faith people view as worth untold fortunes.

That is just how and who we are. We look at things that we can't see knowing that those things require faith in God to obtain. That is why faith people do not see defeat. We don't see failure as an end. We look at things other people would throw away as goods that are worth untold fortunes. That is the same way God looks at us. He looks at us with eyes that cannot see the visible sin and scars of the past that everyone else seems to see so clearly.

God will see a prostitute, a hooker, a woman of the evening and see something totally different than most others see. We might see in her a woman who is promiscuous and represents the low class in society—a moral disgrace. We may see a woman who will never have any prominence or respect in the world that she lives in because of her behavior. Yet, God, on the other hand, sees a woman who is full of faith and power. He sees a person who, once cleansed by the blood of Jesus, will become a world-renowned evangelist winning more people to Jesus than anyone could ever imagine.

Then Joshua son of Nun secretly sent two spies from Shittim. "Go, look over the land," he said, "especially Jericho." So they went and entered the house of a prostitute named Rahab and stayed there (Joshua 2:1 NIV).

Consider Rahab, the harlot of Jericho, who received Joshua's spies into her house. Most religious people would have condemned the men sent to spy out the land. They would have been condemned for being in the company of and lodging with a professing prostitute. Yet, these two men, like God, did not consider the visible; they looked at what they could not see. They saw in her shelter and refuge and protection from the enemy. You can read the entire story in the second chapter of the book of Joshua.

Fortunately for Rahab, the men sent by the king to find out whether or not the spies were staying with her saw her as a prostitute—looking at what they could see. They probably thought that a prostitute was only concerned with earning her wage by providing her services. They did not see her as someone who would believe the voice of God through His servants. They did not see her as someone who could have faith in God's Word.

God saw her totally differently. He looked at Rahab as one who had enormous faith to believe that He would protect her from impending doom. Although she was not a servant of God, and although she was not an Israelite, God's chosen people, she still believed that she and her family would be saved. She believed God's Word. And because of that, Rahab the prostitute was inaugurated into the hall of faith amidst the rich in faith like Noah, Abraham, and Moses.

> *By faith the prostitute Rahab, because she welcomed the spies, was not killed with those who were disobedient* (Hebrews 11:31 NIV).

If God looks beyond the physical, why won't you? It is only when you go beyond the physical realm that you will receive the benefits that are beyond your wildest dreams. Stop looking at where you are now and getting discouraged. Quit worrying about the sin that you committed ten years ago. Don't consider the skills that you lack. Choose to change what you focus on. Start looking at the greater possibilities offered to you in God's Word. Once you do that, you will begin to operate in the faith zone, bringing ultimate pleasure to your Father.

The Power of Focus

> *Brethren, I do not count myself to have apprehended; but one thing I do, forgetting those things*

which are behind and reaching forward to those things which are ahead, I press toward the goal for the prize of the upward call of God in Christ Jesus (Philippians 3:13-14).

The apostle Paul had many wonderful attributes about his character that are very obvious when you read about him in the Bible. He was obviously an educated scholar, having spent many years studying under the tutelage of Gamaliel, a distinguished doctor of the law. He was bold, persistent, and unwavering in his convictions—whether they were right or wrong. He had a wonderful ability to write, having written nearly two-thirds of the New Testament Bible.

Of all his skill, talent, and abilities, I believe that the greatest gift Paul possessed was centered in his ability to focus on the future while simultaneously forgetting his past. This element by itself is what I believe to be the main ingredient for success in a person's walk of faith. You have to let go in order to grasp new realities. Unfortunately, there are many of us who simply cannot seem to just let go of the past and move on. What many people may not know is that it takes faith to let go.

When you really and sincerely believe God's Word concerning where you are going in life, you will not be limited by the few places that you have been. I realize that your past and your present may appear to be more of a reality to you right now than your future. But that's only because you keep on focusing on them.

What you focus on will inevitably become, given the right amount of time. That is why you have to quit focusing on your past. You have to make it your rule that you will always refuse to ponder on the negative words and actions of others. Although it can be difficult at first, you may have to shut negative friends and family members out of your inner circle. You must start believing God to take you to a whole new realm in life. Change your focus!

It takes faith to let go.

Why is it that people tend to focus on their problems more than they do on the solutions? Focusing on your problems will only reward you with greater problems. However, if you focus on the solution, then that is what you will get. In fact, if you focus on the solution long enough, you will become the solution. In the same way, if you focus on Jesus Christ, in time you will become more like Him. In life you will get whatever you focus on.

Focus on the Word of God. Focus on the promises of God. Focus on His provision, His glory, and His presence. In time you will receive a harvest of those things. You really do get what you focus on. I have even heard and witnessed for myself how, over a period of time, a married couple can begin to look like one another because they have become each other's focus.

Wouldn't it be absolutely wonderful to be just like Jesus? Wouldn't it be a sheer joy to walk in faith like many of the biblical patriarchs of old did? It would even be a far greater joy if your life of faith was so pleasing to God that you wrote a chapter in the book of life that others would read and learn from when your life on earth was completed. I'm here to tell you that it is possible. It will become your reality only when you begin to focus on the right thing. Start focusing on the thing that you want to become. You will always get in life what you focus on.

Chapter Three

Great People of Faith

❧

Elijah's Faith-Filled Journey

I sincerely believe in using both biblical and contemporary examples to illustrate my point. So when I think of someone who acted in obedience without having physical proof in order to act, I immediately think of the prophet Elijah. Elijah, whose name means, "My God is Jehovah," lived his entire life fully devoted to pleasing the Lord.

His life's purpose was centered on influencing the apostate and idolatrous people of his time to turn back to God. His mission was to convey the much-ignored message that God is all one, or in other words, that He is *God alone.* This bears great significance in that God has never needed anyone's approval or vote to be God. No person in the world can justify or have to validate His existence. He was God before you arrived here, and He will be God after you are gone.

The old folk used to say it this way: "He's God all by Himself; He don't need nobody's help." Sure enough, that is true. If the church will only come to the knowledge that God can do a perfect job of being God without our input, then we will begin to experience His glory. So Elijah's mission was to get people to see a God whom they could not physically see with their eyes, and believe in Him.

In the spirit, the prophet Elijah foresaw that a drought was coming to devastate that land. This punishment was coming because, contrary to God's desire, King Ahab built a temple in Samaria for people to worship Baal. After Elijah prophesied this word, he quickly fled to the eastern side of the Jordan River and then to Zarepath, which sits on the Mediterranean coast, so he could escape the wrath of the king. Isn't it interesting that this word did not originate with Elijah? He only heard God's word and then conveyed the message to Ahab.

Nevertheless, King Ahab became angry with Elijah, as if he had been the one who was pronouncing the doom. The king should have taken issue with God, not Elijah. However, I am sure that the king knew better than to try and come against the power of God. So he chose to come against God's prophet instead—as if this would be a safer choice. It is obvious that King Ahab did not fully comprehend that God protects His prophets as He would Himself. So if you come against God's prophets, you are coming against God.

> *When they went from one nation to another, and from one kingdom to another people, He permitted no man to do them wrong; yes, He rebuked kings for their sakes, saying, "Do not touch My anointed ones, and do My prophets no harm"* (1 Chronicles 16:20-22).

On both sides of the river God miraculously made provision for Elijah because Elijah simply chose to believe God. This wonderful story of faith opens in 1 King 17 with the prophet declaring the word of the Lord concerning the drought. *"And Elijah the Tishbite, of the inhabitants of Gilead, said to Ahab, "As the LORD God of Israel lives, before whom I stand, there shall not be dew nor rain these years, except at my word"* (verse 1). The first thing we clearly see is that true faith requires you to operate with a spirit of boldness. After all, Elijah was delegated to be the bearer of disturbing news.

How many people do you know who would go up to the king, or president, or prime minister and boldly give him or her a message that you know for sure that leader doesn't want to hear? You probably don't know too many people who would act that boldly. There were so many variables that were connected to Elijah's giving this message. What if it did rain? What if it poured down rain like cats and dogs? This prophet would have been labeled a fraud. Elijah might have been hung for lying to the king.

No matter which way you look at it, Elijah had to have been a great risk taker. If you want to receive the benefits of faith, you, too, will have to be a risk taker. This prophet's faith put him in a position of life and death. However, he knew beyond a shadow of doubt that he had heard the voice of God. It was God's voice alone that gave Elijah the boldness he needed to proclaim this word. When you know that you have heard God, all you have to do is walk in the confidence of what you know.

Faith means taking risks.

No one should ever doubt what he or she knows. If you are male or female, I'm sure you know it. (At least I hope you know it.) No one can convince you otherwise because it is what you know. In the same way Elijah did not have time to wait around hoping to determine whether he had heard from God or not. So by faith he spoke the word of the Lord.

At the end of his prophecy, he told the king that the drought wouldn't stop unless he spoke the word. What's so powerful about this is that here we see God's power working through a vessel that is unafraid to admit that God is actually using him. I am always bothered when I hear wimpy, spineless preachers make continual excuses for the power of God working through them.

They'll say, "I had nothing in the world to do with that healing. There is no power in me whatsoever." What is so pathetic about these kinds of excuses is that they seem to give the impression that we should be afraid to own up to the truth that God can and does use people to get His job done. He uses ordinary people to fulfill His extraordinary purposes in the earth.

If God tells you to pray for someone and that person gets healed, then you did have something to do with it. Your obedience caused the power of God to manifest in that person's life. If you disobeyed God and refused to pray, then your disobedience might have caused someone to die. I believe that people try to hide behind this "excuse curtain" because they are trying to protect God—just in case He messes up. God makes no mistakes. One of the problems that believers run into is this: When we become fearful of acknowledging the power of God working inside us just to pacify unbelievers' expectations of us, we are really denying the power of God.

Having a form of godliness but denying its power. And from such people turn away! (2 Timothy 3:5)

This whole thing of identifying with the Christian faith yet denying the power of the blood and the cross is symptomatic of the perilous times that come during the last days. Neither you nor I have anything to prove to the unbeliever by denying God's power in us. Some people wear the garments of false humility in an attempt to dethrone themselves from the seat that God ordered them to sit in. Thank God Elijah refused to do that. He walked by faith regardless of what people said or thought.

> Then the word of the LORD came to him, saying, "Get away from here and turn eastward, and hide by the Brook Cherith, which flows into the Jordan. And it will be that you shall drink from the brook, and I have commanded the ravens to feed you there" (1 Kings 17:2-4).

Again the Lord spoke to Elijah and told Elijah to turn east and hide at a brook called Cherith. *Cherith* is a word that in the Hebrew means separation, or to cut away. There is an implied lesson in this. Elijah was told by God to hide at this brook, which separated him from the access that Ahab would have had to him if he had stayed where he was.

What does this mean? This means that true faith will cause you to permanently sever ties with doubt, disbelief, and your past, ultimately causing you to become impenetrable to your enemy. Faith protects you from your enemies. Biblical faith puts God on the spot, causing Him to rise to the occasion to show Himself strong and mighty on behalf of His children.

Elijah blindly obeyed the Lord. He began to travel eastward without knowing for sure exactly where he was going. Not once do you hear Elijah asking God for a map, or details, or even what would happen once he arrived. He didn't need any of those things in order to obey. Just God's word alone was enough for the prophet to start moving.

It's interesting to see how Elijah's act of faith caused God's provision to flow into his life and the lives of others. Please understand that God is looking for opportunities to provide for you those things that you cannot provide for yourself. During this time of famine Elijah couldn't provide food for himself. There was no food. God, however, caused ravens to bring food to him.

Faith makes you impenetrable to the enemy.

The mysterious thing is that ravens are scavenger-like birds. They are not the type of birds that share their find with anyone. Yet God used the least likely birds of prey to sustain His servant. In the same way, if you walk by faith and not by sight, God will command the most unlikely people to provide for you. The same people who talked about you, criticized you, and tried to maim your name will be used by God to supply you.

That is one reason why it does not make sense to get all stirred up when people misuse you intentionally. Don't fight them, for that may only delay your blessing. It's best to put them in the hands of God—He knows what's best for them. You'd be shocked at how God can soften the heart of the hardest person, causing him or her to bless you when, before, all he or she did was cause you intentional harm. This only happens, though, when you trust God in faith to provide for you.

Blessed are you when they revile and persecute you, and say all kinds of evil against you falsely for My sake. Rejoice and be exceedingly glad, for great is your reward in heaven, for so they persecuted the prophets who were before you (Matthew 5:11-12).

Faith may take you to places where you were not planning on going to. It also may take you back to a place you just left. The issue is that faith requires believing and obeying God's word, no matter the situation. Sometimes faith may take you into a comfort zone. Other times faith may bring you into the middle of a war zone. Whatever the situation, God will protect you if He sent you there. On the other hand, if God did not tell you to go there, you may be killed. So beware and be careful to know for sure that God is the one prompting you to make the right moves.

Then the word of the LORD came to him, saying, "Arise, go to Zarephath, which belongs to Sidon, and dwell there. See, I have commanded a widow there to provide for you" (1 Kings 17:8-9).

Another faith lesson you need to learn is that you should not get too comfortable with how God did what

He did last time. On the first go round God used ravens to feed Elijah. It would have been a pretty sad situation if Elijah got onto a one-track mind-set and thought that ravens were God's only method of provision. He would have become a lifetime bird watcher.

How God provides for His children will change from time to time. Never get stuck on how He will provide. The thing that should be our focus is the truth that He will provide. Hallelujah! Knowing that alone should get you all excited. You may say, "But I don't know how God's going to get me out of this mess. I don't know how God is going to provide for my bills to be paid. I have no idea how God's going to heal my body. My children have gone so far astray that I really don't know how God will save them." Don't worry about it. Just rejoice in the truth that *God will.* God's methods may change, but His will always remains the same.

A Widow's Faith

So he arose and went to Zarephath. And when he came to the gate of the city, indeed a widow was there gathering sticks. And he called to her and said, "Please bring me a little water in a cup, that I may drink." And as she was going to get it, he called to her and said, "Please bring me a morsel of bread in your hand." So she said, "As the LORD your God lives, I do not have bread, only a hand-

43

ful of flour in a bin, and a little oil in a jar; and see, I am gathering a couple of sticks that I may go in and prepare it for myself and my son, that we may eat it, and die." And Elijah said to her, "Do not fear; go and do as you have said, but make me a small cake from it first, and bring it to me; and afterward make some for yourself and your son. For thus says the LORD God of Israel: 'The bin of flour shall not be used up, nor shall the jar of oil run dry, until the day the LORD sends rain on the earth.' " So she went away and did according to the word of Elijah; and she and he and her household ate for many days (1 Kings 17:10-15).

Have you ever noticed that what is inside the people you spend time with, rubs off on you? For that reason, you should surround yourself with people who live by faith. Their faith will inspire faith in you. That's what happened to the widow here in Zarephath. Elijah's faith affected her faith, and as a result she and her son survived the famine.

Elijah's instructions from God were to go this city where a widow would provide for him. If you walk in faith for very long, you will soon discover that God has a sense of humor. After all, it would be one thing if God commanded a rich woman to take care of Elijah; instead, He had a widow—and obviously a poor widow at that—to provide for the prophet.

Isn't that just like God? He uses the person we think least likely so that He receives the glory, not man. Her lack and destitute state was the perfect avenue for God to perform a miracle. If she had had plenty, God would not have needed to get involved. Instead, just like Jesus did with the five loaves and two fishes, God took the widow's "too little" and turned it into "plenty."

Elijah could have reacted without faith. He could have said, "God, are You joking? This woman has nothing." But perhaps the prophet realized that God was setting this widow up to receive a miracle supply. Either way, Elijah infected this woman with the God-kind of faith— the kind of faith that produces results.

I find it interesting that when the prophet asked this lady to bring him a piece of bread, she immediately gave him a reason for why what she had would not be enough. She told the prophet that she did not have enough food to feed a stray guest. She only had enough for her son and herself. This shows that she did not turn him away out of disrespect or because she did not have a hospitable spirit.

Rather, the famine was so great in the land and she had become so depleted of food that she had determined in her heart that this would be the last meal for herself and her son—and that death would soon follow. For this woman, this was her last supper, a final time for fellow-ship with her child, and she just did not have enough to share with uninvited dinner guests.

Contrary to popular thought, God does not work like we think He should work. Man's carnal thinking would have encouraged this woman to go ahead and eat this last piece of bread with her son—and she would have surely died. God, however, has higher thoughts. When the widow, by faith, released the food out of her hand and placed it in a godly man's hand, God supernaturally caused her oil to begin overflowing and her flour to have a perpetual supply.

The little you hold in your hand is enough to initiate your miracle.

This woman's initial response, however, represents the mind-set that many believers have toward obeying God when that obedience might cost them something tangible. You may give God excuses for why you can't do what He asks you to do. But if God asks you to do it, it's because He knows that you can get the job done. God will never ask you to do what He won't empower you to do. In other words, whatever God asks you to do, He has already made the provision for you to be able to do what He asks. Even though this woman didn't realize it, the little amount that she had in her hand was enough to initiate her miracle.

How much should you give in order to start your miracle process? What is the thing that God has been telling you to do for so long that, once you do it, it will bring blessings into your life? Only you can answer those questions. Whatever that thing is, release your faith in the name of Jesus, obey God, and watch how God will begin to work on your behalf.

Wherever there is potential for blessings to happen, there will always be adverse actions or negative people who will try to convince you to circumvent your blessings. Let's suppose this narrative happened in today's modern godless culture. The story would have read a whole lot differently. Television news shows "60 Minutes" and "Dateline" would have had a field day with this story. They would have made the prophet Elijah look like a preacher who was so careless and so greedy that he took a poor widow's and her son's last meal for his own personal gain. How could a preacher be so insensitive? The headlines in the news would probably read, "False Prophet Profits Off the Poor."

Our judicial system would have tried long and hard to bring criminal charges against him. State legislatures would quickly enact new laws that would protect widowed women, aged women, and single mothers from the influence of preachers, all because of what Elijah did. The public would use his seemingly unkind and selfish act as their justification for why they do not attend church or give money to preachers. They'd say, "All those preachers are the same; all they want is what you have got to give them. They are not concerned about souls; they are just concerned about money and material things."

Admit it, those are the kinds of judgment-casting remarks that you would probably hear. I've only listed a few possible slurs and statements that would be whirled against any present-day preacher who would obey God in faith as Elijah did. Surely you could think of far more negative things that would be said than my short list. Nonetheless, Elijah, in faith, told this woman to do exactly what God said.

Better yet, this woman responded to the prophet's word in complete faith. She could only do this because Elijah had inspired her with his faith in action. It was this faith response that caused supernatural supply to occur (and later provide a miraculous healing for her son). Remember, this woman had already planned to die. She had gotten down to her last meal. The outlook for her future did not look favorable.

So if you really think about it, she didn't have anything to lose. She was as low as she could get. What a truth nugget! When you are as low as you can go, you might as well trust and believe God. Doing so is your only hope. When you operate in biblical faith, you will not always know up front exactly how things will work out. All that you need to know for sure is that God has promised you that it *will* work out. Beware of what people have to say about your choice to obey God.

Most of the time other people will not understand why you do what you do, why you give the sacrificial offering, why you regularly attend church, why you give the tithe, why you fast and pray, why you help the poor and needy, and why you give your last. It's not for them to understand. When God speaks a word into your spirit, God wants you to respond to Him in obedience. The bottom line is that, if it is really God prompting you to do something, there will be fruit that will remain. You will have a significant harvest.

This widow was not much different than any other woman. The Bible does not tell us that she possessed any special powers. It does not say that she walked in any special anointing like Enoch or Elijah. The Bible does not say that she was especially gifted in any area. It does not even say that she walked in the divine favor of the Lord. The one thing this woman did is the same thing you can do: exercise faith.

Anybody can do it. Everybody ought to do it. It does not require special training or skills. All it involves is simply believing God's word. Whether that word comes through a preacher or a child, a sheep or a mule, a rich man or the impoverished, it is still God's word nonetheless. What matters most is that you do not try to qualify His word just because it did not come through the source you are accustomed to.

God still speaks to and through anointed men and women in this day. I believe that these same men and women of God have a word in their mouths for you that, once you heed it, may bring about the change you've been praying for years to come to pass. You see, you don't always need a lot; just use what you have got. It's in your hand!

Blind Man's Faith

Now they came to Jericho. As He went out of Jericho with His disciples and a great multitude, blind Bartimaeus, the son of Timaeus, sat by the road begging. And when he heard that it was Jesus of Nazareth, he began to cry out and say, "Jesus, Son of David, have mercy on me!" Then many warned him to be quiet; but he cried out all the more, "Son of David, have mercy on me!" So Jesus stood still and commanded him to be called. Then they called the blind man, saying to him, "Be of good cheer. Rise, He is calling you." And throwing aside his garment, he rose and came to Jesus. So Jesus answered and said to him, "What do you want Me to do for you?" The blind man said to Him, "Rabboni, that I may receive my sight." Then Jesus said to him, "Go your way; your faith has made you well." And immediately he received his sight and followed Jesus on the road (Mark 10:46-52).

Blind Bartimaeus' story is one of great faith in that he was not a hero in the eyes of his community. Nevertheless, his story deserves honorable mention. He was rather looked down upon as a crippled man always in need of a favor. Despite his very apparent tattered condition, he found the courage to believe God despite what anybody thought about him.

This scriptural narrative swiftly begins by showing how desperately this blind man needed a healing touch from God. His healing was not merely for the sake of being healed; it also meant he would be enabled to function as a normal citizen within his society.

The text opens with an almost unclear picture of Jesus and His disciples coming to Jericho, but for some unknown reason, quickly leaving Jericho. There are many possible reasons Jesus could have come and gone so soon. Perhaps there was an assassination attempt against Jesus. The religious leaders during this era hated the fact that Jesus freely offered His actions of goodwill to the lesser-privileged people. They dubbed Jesus an imposter and a fraud. They falsely thought that Jesus was trying to undermine the religious system of the day. For those reasons they unceasingly sought to kill Jesus.

So it could have been possible that He was avoiding a premature demise. Or, possibly while Jesus was in Jericho, He could not perform miracles because of the people's unbelief. Jesus made a practice of going to places where He would be celebrated, not just tolerated. It was only under these celebratory conditions that Jesus could actually perform miracles. Just as it was during

Jesus' earthly ministry, so it is now. There has to be an attitude of faith and expectation in the people and in the atmosphere in order for healing to happen.

Whatever the reason Jesus came and left Jericho so quickly, we do not know for sure. What we do know is that, as He was leaving the city, He was met at the side of the road by an unassuming character named Bartimaeus.

The text immediately identifies Bartimaeus as the son of Timaeus. The introduction of his father's name is but one more reason for Bartimaeus to embrace an uncompromising faith in Jesus. According to Bible scholars, Timaeus was an unknown man. There is no record that shows Timaeus had any earthly possessions, a place to live, or stature in society.

Plainly stated, this man had no inheritance to leave to his son. Some scholars believe that he, like his son, was also a blind man, bequeathing to his son the spirit and character of a beggar. So it is quite obvious that Bartimaeus started out his life with a potential disadvantage. Being blind would be the obvious disadvantage, but not having an inheritance would be a far greater one. If a rich man in today's society fathered a blind child, the child would not have to worry about having the basic needs of life supplied.

He or she, like other children, would have an opportunity to interact with others. For the most part, the child would be able to live a life as close to normal as anyone would expect. But this man had no mother, no siblings, and no friends to help him. His father, being an unknown figure himself, left no support base for his son to glean from. This left blind Bartimaeus without many choices. He was forced to live a life begging anyone who would see his condition and offer him sympathy and alms.

Within our every disadvantage is the seed of a potential advantage.

One major point that you must understand is this: Whenever there is disadvantage, within that disadvantage is always the seed of a potential advantage. God sets it up that way. This man was blind. He could not see. Since he could not see, he could not make premature judgments based on his sight. What a treasure! This impediment forced this blind man to do what God has been trying to get us to do for ages—walk by faith. *"For we walk by faith, not by sight"* (2 Corinthians 5:7). For most believers, this discipline of walking by faith and not by the sense realm is very difficult to do.

We have been so accustomed to judging people by their educational achievements, their looks, the color of their skin, and the clothes they wear that we have somehow forgotten that it's what is on the inside that matters to God the most. Blind Bartimacus may have been plagued with blindness, but he was blessed with spiritual sight. It was this spiritual sight that caused him to overhear conversations amidst the townspeople about Jesus of Nazareth coming through town. He heard the rumors that this Man named Jesus had supernatural, God-given powers to heal all who were sick and oppressed by the devil. Thank God that this man could hear.

Although most people look down on the vocation of begging, being a beggar does have some advantages. One of those advantages is that you become immune to other people's views and concepts about you. You quickly arrive at the place in life where you really don't care what anyone has to say about you, whether good or bad. The only thing you desire is getting whatever you need. Whether it's food, shelter, or clothing, you become determined to get your needs met, no matter who or how many times you have to ask.

Another up side of being a beggar is that you develop a dogged spirit that never takes "no" for an answer. This was the case with blind Bartimaeus. When he heard about this Man named Jesus who had healed others in recent times past, he could not afford to pass up on the possibility of being healed. Because his hearing was so keen, it would not be a surprise that he also might have heard that Jesus was going to be crucified within a few days. Knowing that information would have made this blind soul far more eager to receive this healing touch, realizing that this might be his only opportunity. How would you respond if you needed a blessing from the Lord, yet you only had one chance at receiving His touch?

Would you, like blind Bartimaeus, do whatever it took to get your blessing? Or would you be afraid of what people might say about you? Would you cower down just to avoid the criticism? Or would you thrive on your critics' remarks, knowing that your miracle was going to happen at any time? I dream of a day when all God's people will gather together and believe God for a miraculous move, one that could not wait until tomorrow. Wouldn't it be fascinating if we went to church with the attitude of, "I am going to praise God as if it were my last time. I need a miracle and I'm not going to leave here until I receive it. If God doesn't touch me today, I may not have a second chance."

When we have this kind of eager motivation, God would be inclined and bound to swiftly answer our prayers. We have to become desperate for a touch from God so that nothing less will satisfy. In the prosperous hour that we live in, we often can become spiritually sidetracked. "Why believe God for healing when I already have a great doctor and good health insurance? Should I really have faith that God will supply my needs? My job seems pretty sure. Do I really need to pray? Things have been going great without my praying. I guess I'll seek God when I get in trouble."

You may not say it that bluntly; however, your attitude and actions may suggest that is how you actually believe. Those who have agreed to walk by faith live in a constant mode of desperation. When we go to God in prayer, we ask with great urgency, making certain that our prayers will not go unnoticed. Blind Bartimaeus heard Jesus walking by the highway and immediately started using his faith. He cried out with a loud voice, *"Jesus, Son of David, have mercy on me!"*

Although the people who were standing by him tried to shut him up, he persisted! *"Son of David, have mercy on me!"* He knew that he could have been arrested for breaching the peace or for being downright obnoxious. But the consequences really did not matter to him. He was focused on one thing and one thing only: He needed to be healed of the thing that had deprived him of freedom for all these years. Nothing was going to stop him from receiving that.

It is interesting to note that the people who stood on the sidelines and heard his cries tried to silence him, yet they had their sight. They could walk wherever they wanted to walk. They worked jobs that required the daily use of their eyes. Yet they did not seem to care that this blind man could not enjoy the vision that they took for granted. Ostracized, scorned, mistreated, and abused, this blind beggar was already conditioned to fight for everything in life that he desired. Until now, he had had to fight for food, a place to lay his head, and torn secondhand clothes to cover his nakedness.

Now the real fight was on. Could it be possible that his impediment so conditioned him to conquer the fight of his life? I think so. This man was conditioned for the fight of faith. He perceived in his spirit that Jesus had the ability to heal him. The only challenge to overcome was getting Jesus to recognize his need. The only tool that he had to do this with was his voice. He could not run toward Jesus for he could not see. If he waved his arms up and down, there was no guarantee that Jesus would be looking in his direction.

Biblical faith begins when you believe that Jesus can and will.

His only hope, his greatest weapon, became his voice. Have you ever thought about using your voice to declare faith's confession? *"Jesus, Son of David, have mercy on me!"* These eight words are so simple, yet so powerful. Eight represents the biblical number of new beginnings. It may very well be possible that these eight words were the only words that needed to be uttered in order for this man to receive his new start.

Jesus could not help but recognize this man's plea. Jesus called Bartimaeus to approach and asked him what his plea was. Even before Bartimaeus could ask Jesus to restore his sight, the healing had already begun. Biblical faith does not begin when the miracle is manifested. It starts when you believe that Jesus can and will do the miracle for you. Having that knowledge alone sets the stage for the miraculous to occur. Jesus confirmed this principle when He told the man, *"Go your way; your faith has made you well."* The result? *"And immediately he received his sight and followed Jesus on the road."*

Just like Abraham, Sarah, and Jacob, that day Bartimaeus received a new name. No longer would the townspeople refer to him as blind Bartimaeus, but simply Bartimaeus. The shackles of blindness had been removed from this hero of faith forever. The stigma associated with his past condition was instantly removed as well. All these things happened when he went against what was normal and decided to take desperate measures to have faith in the only One who could permanently set him free—Jesus Christ.

How about you? Are you ready for a name change? Are you ready to receive your healing? You have been sick for far too long now. You have accepted poverty and lack as a lifestyle for far too long. You don't have to settle for living on a low spiritual plane. Bartimaeus is an example worth following. Use the voice of the Lord within you to activate your faith. Say what blind Bartimaeus said. Say it with the same spirit and conviction with which he said it. Say it loud! Proclaim it boldly! Keep repeating it until it becomes real to you. Say it now and get results.

"Jesus, Son of David, have mercy on me! Jesus, Son of David, have mercy on me! Jesus, Son of David, have mercy on me!"

Chapter Four

More Great People of Faith

Uriah's Faith

In most church circles, preachers and writers have been known to totally exhaust the topics that discuss the biblical figures known for being strong in faith, possessing unusual loyalty, and tapping into the miraculous arena. So for the most part, when faith is mentioned, people automatically think of the obvious faith men and women such as Abraham, who is called the father of faith and who was willing to sacrifice Isaac, his son of promise, on an altar.

They think about Elijah and how he used his faith in God to resurrect a widow's dead child. Many people remember how, by faith, Noah built an ark to protect a remnant of God's people from the deadly effects of the flood. Isaac blessed Esau and Jacob and spoke forth their destinies by faith. By faith Jacob had his name changed to Israel after an encounter with God, and so on. These examples are the obvious ones.

Very rarely do we explore beyond the obvious to discover the lesser-known, lesser-mentioned people in the Bible who exerted just as strong, if not stronger, feats of faith as the better-known ones. That is why I feel that Uriah deserves honorable mention in this chapter. Uriah's story is colorfully told in the book of 2 Samuel the eleventh chapter. Before Uriah enters the scene, though, there are a few things that happen.

First, David, who was king and who should have been at the battleground giving directions, had stayed at home. Because David was not where he was supposed to be, it opened the door for the enemy to fill David's time with pleasurable pursuits that were far beyond his boundary as a king. You see, one day David saw a beautiful woman by the name of Bathsheba bathing. He was so taken and overwhelmed by her outward beauty and presence that he decided to pursue her.

He asked his messenger to go and get this woman at once. Although he was told that she was a married woman, his immediate desire for pleasure seemed far greater than anything else. Temporarily ignoring his call and common sense, he had an affair with Bathsheba and got her pregnant. Knowing that her pregnancy would have caused widespread rumors and possible impeachment, King David's heart began to fill up quickly with fear. Fear, no matter how you look at it, will always hinder faith's progress.

Overcome by fear, David came up with what he thought was a foolproof plan. Realizing that Bathsheba's husband would soon return home from the battlefield, he arranged for Bathsheba and her husband Uriah to spend some alone time together. He figured that Uriah would surely desire to sleep with his wife after working so tirelessly at war. And if Uriah slept with his wife, then the child would appear to be his and not the king's when the baby finally arrived. The plan seemed sure.

Enter Uriah...

When Uriah had come to him, David asked how Joab was doing, and how the people were doing, and how the war prospered. And David said to Uriah, "Go down to your house and wash your feet." So Uriah departed from the king's house, and a gift of food from the king followed him. But Uriah slept at the door of the king's house with all the servants of his lord, and did not go down to his house. So when they told David, saying, "Uriah did not go down to his house," David said to Uriah, "Did you not come from a journey? Why did you not go down to your house?" And Uriah said to David, "The ark and Israel and Judah are dwelling in tents, and my lord Joab and the servants of my lord are encamped in the open fields. Shall I then go to my house to eat and drink, and to lie with my wife? As you live, and as your soul lives, I will not do this thing." Then David said to Uriah, "Wait here today also, and tomorrow I will let you depart." So Uriah remained in Jerusalem that day and the next (2 Samuel 11:7-12).

Uriah totally upset the king's plan. His faith and faithfulness to fight, defend, and protect the honor and posterity of the king was unmatched. True faith is always focused. Biblical faith cannot be easily distracted. It is so focused that it will delete anything that does not help its cause. Uriah believed that his contribution to join in battle against the enemy would bring about a significant victory for his kingdom. He realized that his battalion could have possibly been wiped out if he lost his focus for even one moment.

"Why was Uriah a man of great faith?" I am glad you asked. Most people look at faith in terms of great feats or huge acts of courage. You must accept that faith is real, faith is tangible, and faith is substance. Although faith is something that we can see, the results of faith are not always recognized with our physical eyes. There are some people whom God clearly labels as being men and women of great faith even though they did not have anything to prove it like Noah had the ark and young David had a sling and stones.

There are some acts of faith and qualities of faith that remain inward. That's called character. I'm sure you would agree that in the hour in which we live, character is something that few people embrace and the masses shun. Uriah had both tremendous character and faith. This faith caused him to make a commitment to the king, one that he would not renege on no matter what. In the day in which we live, people tend to be so gun-shy when it comes to commitment. This is the reason some may have a hard time comprehending why Uriah would persevere under opposing conditions.

Why is it that a man will live with a woman whom he is not married to for ten years, yet when she questions why he won't marry her, he becomes frustrated? I'll tell you why: He's afraid to commit. Why is it that a person will visit a local church for one or more years, yet when the pastor kindly asks that individual to join, he or she doesn't show up anymore? That person doesn't want to commit. Why did a man named Jonah choose not to preach to a city that God specifically told him to preach deliverance to? He could not see himself committing, particularly to do something that he really did not want to do.

The examples could go on and on. The point is that it takes great faith to make a choice to commit. When you commit, you are saying that you have willingly chosen to abort any other options. There are no other viable choices in this matter, except to go forward. When people run from church to church, they have not made a genuine commitment.

If they had, then hopping from one church to the next wouldn't be an option for them. They may say, "People gossip and cause too much trouble in that church." They ignorantly think that they will find a church where people are "opinion-less." There is no such church. No matter where you go, people will always be people. That is the truth that you will just have to face. It's all a part of growing up spiritually.

It takes great faith to make a choice to commit.

When a test or trial comes in the church life of the faithful and committed, that is when they will stand up, search for solutions, and begin to fight like good soldiers should. Why? Once you have made a truly faith-based decision, you can't look back. It's impossible. Every door has been closed, so the only way out is to go through. Now that is faith in action!

Many people choose not to commit in faith because they do not know for sure what the outcome of their commitment will be. If everybody knew exactly for sure what they where going to have to endure when they got married, perhaps half of the married world would still be unmarried. People who commit to serve in the United States Armed Forces don't commit expecting the worst, even though the worst could possibly happen.

They go in with an optimistic viewpoint and believe God for the best results: few defeats and many victories. If we know in advance what will happen, then we will not have a genuine need for faith. Faith only works in situations where we really don't know what the outcome is going to be. However, we willingly put our faith in God, trusting that He will ultimately see us through the process safely.

Although King David was trying to redirect Uriah's attention toward his wife, Uriah steadfastly kept his eyes on what he was faithfully committed to do. He suspected not a thing. He had no idea that the king was devising a wicked plan that would ultimately cause him to die on the battlefield. The king, in whom Uriah put all of his confidence, would soon betray him, sending him to the front line of the battlefield to be treacherously murdered.

*The archers shot from the wall at your servants;
and some of the king's servants are dead, and
your servant Uriah the Hittite is dead also*
(2 Samuel 11:24).

This same king who had riches untold and noble status stole one commoner's only true possession: his wife. Yes, the king stole his wife and devised a plan to take his life, but in all this he still remained faithfully committed to his call to defend the nation. How would you view such a death? Do you see it as a horrible death or one of great merit and honor? I choose to believe that Uriah died with great honor.

He went to his resting place believing that his faith would be rewarded if he kept his word to fight to the end. A faith like his should become an icon for believers everywhere of how true commitment should look. Faith to commit should never be predicated on circumstances or situations. "I'll commit if this or that happens." "I'll stay committed only as long as you do this or that." "If you ever get in trouble, then it's over."

A person who lives by the faith code, which simply states, "I'll believe no matter what," should never utter statements such as these. What if Jesus takes longer to return than you expected He would? Will you stop serving Him, or are you in this for the long haul? What if your finances seem to be diminishing, yet you are faithfully tithing and giving offerings? Will you quit giving altogether?

What if your husband won't act right, or your wife just won't do right—is that a just cause for ignoring your vows to each other? I think not. Faith to commit means that you will do "by faith" what your heart and your spoken word has promised to do. I pray that you will embrace the faith that Uriah possessed to fight and win. His character and commitment are enough by themselves to proclaim Uriah the winner that he is and will always be remembered as.

Jack Coe, Sr.—A Man of Reckless Faith

Although biblical characters serve as guides for the Christian believer, God still uses people today to display

His matchless power. As far as requirements are concerned, God only looks for people who are willing to operate by faith. My father, the late great Jack Coe, Sr., was such a man. He was truly a man of reckless faith. By this I mean that my father never considered the consequences of his actions if he knew for sure that God was telling him to do something.

He knew that God would protect his interests. Dad was a bold and fearless man. I never remember my father being afraid of lawyers, politicians, or police officers. He fearlessly refuted negative reports from doctors and stood boldly before judges, declaring his faith in God's Word. In my lifetime, I have seen a lot of great faith preachers and healers. However, I have not met anyone with the amount of personal conviction that God could do anything like my dad had.

Whether believing for God to supply a $100,000 need (during a time when $100,000 was worth about $2 million in today's money), or believing God to cause sight to come to a blinded eye, bring hearing to a deaf ear, and feed, clothe, and shelter several hundred children passing through his orphanage, he knew that God would do it. Although my father respected the law and was a law-abiding citizen, he was never afraid of being arrested or put in jail simply because he did what God told him to do.

If you are going to really follow Jesus, you can't be afraid of the systems of this world. One of the things that will prohibit you from living a lifestyle of faith is trying so hard to be compliant with a worldly system. Jesus never did, and neither should you. I am often amazed, yet saddened, by how many ministers try to become mainstream in their theology while factoring Jesus totally out of the equation. If you are going to walk by faith, you have got to remember that you were not called to be like everybody else; neither were you called to be compliant to a godless system. You were called to obey God, confront injustice, and bring about change.

If you are going to really follow Jesus, you can't be afraid of the systems of this world.

My father demonstrated his bold faith in 1956 when, while preaching revival services in Miami, Florida, he was arrested by the police. The power of God was so mighty during these services and so many miracles and healings were taking place that it shook the community—as well as the devil. So he tried to stop what was happening.

People in the community alleged that my father was practicing medicine without a license, which is illegal. That was totally false, of course. Like any minister who believes the Bible concerning healing, my dad laid his hands on the sick and believed that Jesus would heal them. My dad was never afraid to cast the devil out of people who were possessed with demon spirits, as the scripture says to believers in Mark 16:17-18:

And these signs will follow those who believe: In My name they will cast out demons; they will speak with new tongues; they will take up serpents; and if they drink anything deadly, it will by no means hurt them; they will lay hands on the sick, and they will recover (Mark 16:17-18).

Knowing that he had God's Word as the basis for his actions and his obedience, Dad feared not what man would do to him. There were many preachers then and even far more now who would have gotten out of the healing ministry altogether had this kind of pressure come against them.

I know for certain that when your ministry is truly a God-ordained ministry, it will suffer persecution by those who don't know Jesus. True Christian ministry will always put you in a controversial position. And that position is where my dad constantly lived. It seems quite ridiculous that these people would charge my father with practicing medicine without a license, particularly when he never used any drugs on the people he was praying for. He never prescribed any medication.

Our spiritual enemy, the devil, was getting desperate. He knew how Dad's bold faith in Jesus would spread to everyone who heard the Gospel. He had to shut down those services! So some atheistic groups, and even church denomination officials, trumped up these false charges.

Now, my dad had a brash kind of sense of humor. There were times when the local newspaper reporters would get comments from him. Dad wasn't shy about giving comments; neither was he afraid of the potential for lies and false reporting that they were accustomed to printing. He'd tell them, "Just make sure that when you print my name you spell it right. That's JACK COE!"

He even used their negative publicity to his advantage. He knew well that people would respond to negative publicity with more fervor than positive publicity. Anything or any method that he could use to catapult his Gospel meetings, he would use. It really didn't matter what anyone thought about him; Dad was far more concerned about whether Jesus got the glory or not and if His children were walking in health.

The arresting police put him behind bars. They then released him on a $5,000 bond and a promise to appear for his court hearing.

When he was released, my dad contacted friends from across the nation to come and testify on his behalf. Sadly, many refused, afraid that the negative exposure would affect their own ministries or churches. Fortunately, many others who also believed in divine healing did travel to Florida to stand up for my father in court—men of stature like Gordon Lindsey, founder of Christ for the Nations, and Raymond Richey, a world-famous healing evangelist.

God prevailed at the hearing, and the judge dismissed the case. The judge could not in good conscience charge my father who, in "good faith," tried to usher Christ's healing power to anyone who would believe.

The rich in faith make the choice to do it God's way, or they don't do it at all.

Sometimes I wonder how things might have turned out if my father had been a coward. What if he became compliant with the system just to satisfy the atheists and some godless churchgoers? How would his ministry have ended? Personally, I don't believe that you can fail if you follow God's path. And His path is clearly written out in His Word. However, it takes great faith to follow it because God's Word is not necessarily pleasing to every ear that hears it. So the rich in faith make the choice to do it God's way, or they don't do it at all. Despite constant attacks against his ministry, my dad chose to do it God's way.

I know a lot of ministers and ministries today, but I don't think any of them attracted as much or more criticism than my father's did. All the while, though, my dad kept his faith in God. He believed God for everything. And God continually proved Himself faithful. Jack Coe, Sr., would set up big gospel tents all around America in major cities and in small towns and preach salvation and healing in Jesus' name. He would go wherever God told him to go.

My father, also by faith, hosted racially integrated meetings. Now this was during the time of high racial tension; after all, it was the 1950's. If you were to pull out some of the old footage of those meetings, you would see both black and white ministers sitting on the platform. You also would see both black and white brothers and sisters worshipping together in the audience. I'm pretty sure there were people in the audience who did not approve, but Dad didn't care about their opinions.

You might think, "What's the big deal? That's how it was supposed to be, anyway." Yes, that is how things should have always been, but it wasn't how it was. Many ministers during this same era were afraid to confront the ills and racial divisions within society. Rather than fight or believe God for a change, most of the ministers back then went along with the status quo. They would rather have been safe than risky.

Biblical faith will, at times, cause you to become reckless. When you are surely operating with the same faith that Jesus was charged with, you don't care about status quo or trying to fit in. All you are concerned with is pleasing God. You only want His approval. Truthfully speaking, you will often disappoint many when you purpose in you heart to obey God in faith. Did my dad defy the laws of the land? Yes! He defied any law that was in direct opposition to God's law. God's law said:

But He was wounded for our transgressions, He was bruised for our iniquities; the chastisement for our peace was upon Him, and by His stripes we are healed (Isaiah 53:5).

Since God's law said that we should enjoy the benefit of divine healing, my dad would willingly confront or even break any law that would prohibit this freedom in Christ. Although Jim Crow laws were prevalent in the Southern states and their poisonous effects spilled over even into many Northern states, my father was reminded of God's law concerning the matter.

Concerning racial issues, God's law was totally opposite to common law at that time; therefore, he had to choose between the law of the land and God's law. Although it would make him an enemy of the system and other fellow ministers did not agree with his choice, Dad still chose God's law. He knew what God's Word said about the matter concerning division with races of people. Since God did not like it, neither did he.

And He has made from one blood every nation of men to dwell on all the face of the earth, and has determined their preappointed times and the boundaries of their dwellings, so that they should seek the Lord, in the hope that they might grope for Him and find Him, though He is not far from each one of us; for in Him we live and move and have our being, as also some of your own poets have said, "For we are also His offspring" (Acts 17:26-28).

They Died Believing

These all died in faith, not having received the promises, but having seen them afar off were assured of them, embraced them and confessed that they were strangers and pilgrims on the earth (Hebrews 11:13).

Most of the time, when you read books about faith, many authors conveniently forget to mention that there were some people who died in faith, believing that God would fulfill His promise, yet who never physically received it. You may have had a Christian relative, a mother or father, a sister or brother who died from a drawn-out illness, yet while that loved one was alive, he or she sincerely believed with all of his or her heart that God would heal him or her.

Why do some people die? What actually happened? Did they really believe God? Were they really standing in faith? I believe that we need to look into this matter a little further. There is a group of believers who believe that if you are in faith, you cannot die. They say your faith will keep you alive forever, no matter what. A totally different group ascribes to a different train of thought. They believe that whether you have faith or not, your time to die is just your time to die.

Which side should you believe? Here is one truth that you should realize. Although it pleases God to respond to our actions of faith, it is ultimately His call on whether or not we will receive the promise that we were expecting. Now don't misunderstand me. I am not giving anyone an excuse not to operate in and by faith because God will do whatever He wants to do anyway. That is not what I am saying. What I am saying is this: *Your faith moves God's heart and His hand. It always has and it always will.*

However, there are some situations where God has to override what we think is best for us for His ultimate glory. In order to understand this, you'll have to see the bigger picture. Unfortunately, at times we can only see the smaller picture. We can only see where we are right now and the limited impact that we are making. But there are certainly times when we have to simply trust God and believe that what He chooses to allow is for our ultimate benefit.

Your faith moves God's heart and His hand. It always has and it always will.

At the height of his ministry, my father died. It was a total shock to the whole church world, especially to those who led successful healing ministries. Daddy was only 38 years old when he died, obviously a young man with a growing family and a ministry that was set to do greater things than any ministry had ever done before. Just before his death, my father was in place to set the pace for television evangelism long before many of the evangelists who air freely today.

In many ways I view my dad as a trailblazer. He plowed out territory that other ministries coming after him can now enjoy. When the faithful died believing for the promise, *the promise* did not have to necessarily come through them. But their *faith* involvement set the stage for the promise to become a reality. I see my father in this light. Although he saw great miracles and healing campaigns in his ministry, he sowed so that those who would come after him would see even greater miracles than he did.

Faith that'll take a lickin' is faith that keeps on ticking, keeps on moving even after you are dead. People many generations after you have died will benefit from your life of faith now. For example, I have traveled to hold healing meetings in the Ukraine and Russia, places that my father could not go when he was alive because they were not open for Christian believers to minister there.

His promise from God was that, through his life, many people would come to know Jesus and be healed in His name. Now that promise is alive in his offspring. Glory to God! Maybe he didn't receive the promise to realize in his lifetime, but the promise did not die just because his flesh died. Just as there were many in the Scriptures who died in faith and did not receive a physical promise during their lifetimes, the promise was yet bound to live in the people whom they touched with their vision.

After all, Jesus died. No one can tell me that Jesus did not die in faith. Because He died in faith, the resurrected spirit of Christ now lives in every believer. So whatever promises that Jesus did not actualize while He walked this earth, He will see them done through His children. That alone should be a tremendous encouragement to you.

The renowned faith healer Kathryn Kuhlman died before she physically saw the promises of her ministry. Yet her ministry lives on in the ministries and hearts of those whom she touched. Pastor Benny Hinn is one of many lives that have been touched by her ministry. Publisher, author, educator, and leader in the healing movement Gordon Lindsay died never having witnessed the unfathomable outreach and soul-winning power of Christ For The Nations Institute. However, his wife, Frieda Lindsay, has done a remarkable job of raising up young missionaries with the message of Christ to the nations of the world. You see, the promise to him lives on.

Evangelist A.A. Allen infused his young pupil, R.W. Schambach, with such a desire to heal the sick that where Allen finished, Brother Schambach took over and has reached tremendous heights in ministry. *These all died in faith.* This simply says that you cannot lose if you are in faith. It's impossible! It's great to live in faith, but it's just as great to die in faith. If you didn't see the promise in your lifetime, don't worry. God will carry His promises, His healing power, His saving grace, and His deliverance through those whom you touched in love. Even in death you still win, when you are walking by faith!

"O Death, where is your sting? O Hades, where is your victory?" The sting of death is sin, and the strength of sin is the law. But thanks be to God, who gives us the victory through our Lord Jesus Christ. Therefore, my beloved brethren, be steadfast, immovable, always abounding in the work of the Lord, knowing that your labor is not in vain in the Lord (1 Corinthians 15:55-58).

Writing in Your Name

One of the wonderful things about God is that He gives equal opportunity to anyone who will dare to believe. Whether you were a great healing evangelist or not really does not matter. You, too, can be on God's list of "Faith's Hall of Fame." All you have to do is write your name in. God is not a respecter of persons. However, He is a great respecter of principles. Faith is not only a law, but it is also a principle that must be practiced on a regular basis in order to receive its maximum benefit.

By using your faith and acting on God's Word, you, too, will write in your name as one of those who lived by faith. For me, this has become one of my lifetime goals; it's the vision that I am possessed with. Whether I am caught up to meet Christ in the air or if I die and am then resurrected, I want to leave a legacy behind on this earth. When I speak of legacy, I am speaking of something far greater in value than money, far greater than houses and lands, and far greater than fancy cars.

I want to leave a legacy of faith to everyone who is left on this earth. I want people to read about how I used my faith in God and toward God to do mighty works and great exploits in Jesus' name. My life will be considered a success if others can use my example as a sort of blueprint that will guide them step by step on how to live by faith, believing God for everything and moving mountains.

The good news is that God is signing people up on a rolling admission basis. No matter how old you are, it's not too late. Remember that Abraham was a hundred years old when he received his promised son by faith. On the other hand, you are not too young. *"Josiah was eight years old when he became king, and he reigned thirty-one years in Jerusalem"* (2 Kings 22:1a). All you have to do is just show up. Show up ready and willing to do whatever God says, go wherever He wants you to journey, pray for whomever He tells you to pray for, and say whatever He commands you to speak. If you show up with this attitude, you, like me, can just write in your name of great people of faith. Go ahead; do it now by faith.

Great People of Faith

_____

Your Name

Chapter Five

Your Faith Must Withstand Testing

༺✿༺

Behold, I have refined you, but not as silver; I have tested you in the furnace of affliction (Isaiah 48:10).

There is one thing you need to know about faith that will last. And that is this: Your faith will be tested. Now I fully realize that you may not want to hear anything about going through tests. After all, for most people, life has been one series after another of taking tests. For the most part, people generally don't get too excited when they know that a test is coming their way.

One of the main reasons for why people are not very much excited about tests is because they know that there is always a possibility of failing the test. And when that happens, you have to take the test all over again. That can be a bit discouraging. Now if the test you were given as a retake came in the identical way as the one you failed, it would probably be a whole lot easier for you to pass the second time around.

Unfortunately, that is not what usually happens. You fail one test, but the retake is often totally different. It can be so different that you may actually wonder for a moment if this test applies to the same class. God is not concerned about your ability to memorize just enough to get a passing grade. He wants you to master this stuff we use called faith. Mastery, however, only prepares you for yet another test of faith—but on a far higher level of intensity.

So what now? You realize that if your faith is going to be strong and stand the test of time, you will have to endure some test under the most stringent measures. You may ask, "Brother Coe, what if I just can't pass? What if I don't have what it takes to endure this test? Maybe this test will kill me. Then what will the test have been worth?" One thing you must realize is that the tests God allows to come your way are not for the purpose of killing you or destroying you.

Therefore let him who thinks he stands take heed lest he fall. No temptation has overtaken you except such as is common to man; but God is faithful, who will not allow you to be tempted

beyond what you are able, but with the tempta-
tion will also make the way of escape, that you
may be able to bear it (1 Corinthians 10:12-13).

When God brings tests, they come as tools to refine us in the furnace that is life. God, in His own special way, uses tests as a measurement tool to gauge exactly how much character we really have. It's the character within each of us that God is primarily concerned with developing. Blessings come easy and can be easily lost. However, your truest character qualifies you to receive whatever heights of greatness that are humanly imaginable.

Brother Job Passed His Test

The book of Job chronicles the life story of a hero of faith. A question that puzzles many, though, is this. If Job was such a great man of faith, why then did he go through all that suffering? Surely such great faith would mean that he shouldn't go through the trials and tests that he did. The answer is that *the way* Job endured those tests and trials validated his faith in God *and* God's faith in him. Notice that I said that God had faith in Job.

You know you have reached the apex of your faith walk when God can recommend you as one of His tro-phies. God's recommendation stands alone. For if God recommends you, know that He also has pre-equipped you with everything necessary to complete the tasks that

83

He volunteered you for. Remember that God equips those whom He chooses. If you go through a test or trial, then you can know that God gave you what you need to go through that trial before it occurred.

> *Then the LORD said to Satan, "Have you considered My servant Job, that there is none like him on the earth, a blameless and upright man, one who fears God and shuns evil?" So Satan answered the LORD and said, "Does Job fear God for nothing? Have You not made a hedge around him, around his household, and around all that he has on every side? You have blessed the work of his hands, and his possessions have increased in the land. But now, stretch out Your hand and touch all that he has, and he will surely curse You to Your face!" And the LORD said to Satan, "Behold, all that he has is in your power; only do not lay a hand on his person." So Satan went out from the presence of the LORD (Job 1:8-12).*

Think about it. How would you feel if you knew that God was having a deep conversation about you with the devil? Just the thought of that makes me quiver. Although I know that God is a good God, I, too, know that there is no goodness in the devil at all. And even though I know that God won't permit the devil to overtake my life, I still would not feel quite settled just knowing that the devil was up to something no good concerning me.

84

The only thing worse than knowing that the devil is talking to God about me is if I were totally uninformed that they have agreed on new, drastic rearrangements for my life. It almost seems like someone was talking behind my back while not in my presence. That makes me feel very uncomfortable, primarily because I do not have any say so in the matter.

If I were present at the negotiations, I would periodically make suggestions to both God and the devil to go a little easy on me. I'd make sure that they kept in mind that the pain that will be endured would be pain that *I'm* going to feel, not them. I would make sure that they fully understood that so they would exercise some compassion on an innocent soul. Problem was, Job did not have the privilege of knowing what was going on. His ignorance of his coming trial put him at a total disadvantage. He became totally vulnerable to his environment. Worse yet is that Job was totally unprepared for everything that was getting ready to happen to him.

I encourage you to take the time and read the entire book of Job. At first it appears to concentrate on the suffering of a victimized righteous man. But as you continue to read, you will suddenly discover that Job is really not the main character in his self-titled book, but rather God. God's wisdom and providence clearly become far greater than Job's temporary pain and tragic loss. You will see God as the main theme all throughout this wonderful book.

The book of Job shows the Christian believer how God allows situations to become a reality for the greater purpose of exercising one's faith and proving God faithful over and over again. Job gets the bad news that all his ten children were killed by a freak storm. That news alone is enough to make a strong man mentally snap. If Job conquered the tragedy of losing his children and nothing else, he would have still earned merit in the eyes of God and man. Most people would not hold up under the very real pressure of that kind of loss. However, Job did not snap. He stayed strong.

Some situations have the greater purpose of exercising your faith and proving God faithful.

Satan continually tries to see what tactic he can use to get you to lose your mind. If he can't get you one way, he will get you another. You see, that wasn't the first thing that happened. No, messengers came to tell Job that all his livestock were either stolen and killed, and his servants murdered. Basically Job's businesses, his staff, and all his real estate holdings were suddenly no more. He lost his entire business empire and family in one day due to the devil's handiwork.

Can you imagine how you would respond if this happened to you? I did not even bother asking how you would feel because I obviously already know the answer to that question. Just think how trapped this God-fearing man must have felt. Far beyond that feeling, though, he must have felt somewhat betrayed by God.

Why would God allow these horrible things to happen to an innocent man? Does God even care about His people? Does God get pleasure when we hurt and suffer? If not, then why doesn't He just stop all suffering? It seems like the good people in life always get the short end of the stick. These questions and thoughts all represent common human reasoning and understanding. In the midst of trials we often ask questions that center on what we are going through at that moment. Although we are the ones who suffer at times, the focus really should not be on us. Focusing on self will only drain us emotionally, mentally, financially, and spiritually.

If you have already gone as low as you can in life, why focus on your condition? That will never make things change. Instead of asking why, how, and "does God" questions, you should more appropriately ask who. Once Moses complained to God that he was unable and ill-equipped to speak on behalf of the enslaved children of Israel. God then reminded him of *who* He is. He told him, "I am who I am." In other words, whatever you need from God at any point in your life, He already is what you need.

God does not have to become what you need; He already is. That is who God is. Although it seemed like Job was faced with pressures that he would not be able to bear, he had to constantly remind himself of who actually was in charge. You lost your home, but God's in charge. You lost your marriage or your children to drugs and crime, yet God is still in charge. You nearly lost your mind, but by the grace of God He reminded you that He is still in charge of your mind.

This is the key to your lasting and staying strong in faith no matter what. This is how your faith will withstand every test. Your endurance comes when you realize and accept the truth that, no matter what happens in life, God is and always will be in charge. Job was human just like you are. He was not supernatural. He only believed in a supernatural God who could help him to endure subhuman calamities. God knows that you have a breaking point and will not allow you to go through more than you can bear.

How will you pass your test? You will pass only when you put in the forefront of your thinking that God has already made a way for you to escape. If God chooses not to make a way for you to escape, then He will strengthen you to be able to withstand the attack. Either way, you will not have to draw from the empty well of your own strength.

You can fully rely on the unlimited supply of the strength of the Lord. After Job came to accept all that had happened and recognized that he was unable to do anything to change or fix what had transpired, he chose to worship the Lord. In other words, he began to tell God how much He was worth to him. Through his worship he was imparted strength enough to be described in the following:

In all this Job did not sin nor charge God with wrong (Job 1:22).

Knowing *who* to charge is also key to having lasting faith. I am always bothered when I hear people say things like, "God killed my mother or father." "God took my children away from me." "God let me lose my house." "God does not love me." And so on. It is so unfair to charge God with any of these atrocities. God is not a killer or a thief. He is not a destroyer of families. Rather, He is the personification of Love itself.

When your focus is not where it should be, however, you will tend to charge God with crimes that the devil should do the time for. Job knew not to charge God with wrong, for charging God with wrong is a sin. Let's face it; the devil has got off the hook for far too long now. He has framed God thousands of times over and it's just not right. If the devil did the crime, then let's expose that joker. Let the world know just how evil and wicked your adversary really is.

Even though Job could not make much sense of what was happening, he still knew not to charge God with the evil that was happening to him. He knew that somehow God would again prove Himself faithful as He had in the past. Not for one moment would Job give Satan the benefit or the leeway to believe that faith in God was unprofitable. He passed the test. And because he did, God restored him in every way far beyond his original net worth.

God did not have to restore Job's self-worth because Job never lost that. He knew who he was in God. Just knowing that will always remind you of how much you are really worth. You'll recognize that, with or without things, you are priceless in the eyes of the Lord. Although Job showed obvious signs of fatigue, he never quit. He never gave up. He never stopped believing God. Job passed the test. Will you, too, pass the test?

> Now the LORD blessed the latter days of Job more than his beginning; for he had fourteen thousand sheep, six thousand camels, one thousand yoke of oxen, and one thousand female donkeys. He also had seven sons and three daughters (Job 42:12-13).
>
> After this Job lived one hundred and forty years, and saw his children and grandchildren for four generations. So Job died, old and full of days (Job 42:16-17).

My Personal Battle With Colon Cancer

More than 20 years ago, God healed me miraculously of cancer. I can never forget the day when I found out that I had cancer. I couldn't believe it. Neither did I want to accept it. I'm pretty sure that you know cancer is one of those diseases most everyone dreads. I had known of friends and even had relatives who had cancer. Some even died of this horrible disease. One thing I did know was that

I was a young man and it was not my time to go, for the simple reason that God was not through with me yet.

In fact, I felt as if God was just getting started with me. I believed for souls to be won to Jesus all over this world. I could not do this if my body continued to break down because of the cancer. The colon, which is where my cancer was, is the place where your body gets all of its vitamins and nutrients. If my colon was cancerous, it would not only affect my colon area, but eventually my entire body. I went for treatments in an attempt to alleviate myself of this disease. Although the treatments helped some, they did not rid me of the cancer.

Quickly, I had gotten to the point where I had become dissatisfied with my progress. I had so much to do, so many places to go, and untapped ministry lying within myself that I became dissatisfied with my life. For years I had taught people all over the country about the God of the Bible. I had taught them that with God nothing is impossible. Over and over again I reminded the saints that all things are possible if only you believe. Now I found myself facing a real life-and-death situation. What was I to do?

I made the choice to pass this test. The only alternative to passing this test would be to die, and I was not about to give in to that. I would not confess my cancerous condition. Although I knew that the cancer was in my body and although I felt weak and was often in pain, I would not confess what I was feeling. I began to realize more than ever that if I continued to confess what I was feeling, I would get more pain.

So I started to confess what I desired. I desired to be healed. I wanted to be cured of cancer. I wanted to live a wonderful, happy, and productive life with my beautiful wife. I wanted to see my grandchildren grow up and be an active part of their lives. None of these things would have ever been if I had focused on my pain. Every day, I would say, "I am healed in Jesus' name. My body is cancer-free. I am healthy and whole. I will spend many years married to and loving on my wife Frieda, my gift from God. I will not die prematurely. Thousands, then millions, of people will come to know the Lord Jesus as I preach the name of Jesus all over the world. I'll see my grandchildren grow up to adulthood. I'll spend quality time with my children and my grandchildren. We will go on family trips to Disney World and other parts of the country together."

It was these confessions that were made in Jesus' name, or in other words, using His authority, that brought me through. My test began to intensify when I would make these confessions, yet my situation did not seem to get better as quickly as I thought it should have. There were times when I felt in my flesh that I should stop believing. *Maybe it's not worth it. I am confessing and believing, yet I am getting worse.*

Thanks to God I did not give in to my flesh. My spirit overrode the will of my flesh, and I continued to believe for my healing. After a while, my confessions in Jesus' healing power paid off. I was completely healed of the cancer and it has never reoccurred since. Was it easy?

92

Not at all. It was probably one of the hardest tests that I had endured at the time. Was it worth it? Without a doubt, it was well worth it.

As with any test, you should come away having learned a valuable lesson. You should have tools that will carry you through your next journey. The lesson that I learned was that *God is faithful.* That might seem a little bit elementary to you. However, you would be surprised to discover how many churchgoers don't realize that God is faithful. Knowing that has increased my faith to do things in this earth like never before. I think like this: *If God healed me of cancer, there is nothing that He won't do for me.*

I learned that God is faithful.

If I have faith to believe God for an automobile, a house, a church building, an office complex, to save a million souls through my preaching the Word, to establish churches and Bible colleges on the foreign mission field, or to keep me disease-free, I know He will. If God did it once, He will do it again. Ever since I passed the test with cancer, God has proved Himself faithful in all these areas that I have mentioned, more than once. He will continue to keep proving Himself if I continue to trust Him.

Even Jesus Was Tested

Then Jesus was led up by the Spirit into the wilderness to be tempted by the devil. And when He had fasted forty days and forty nights, afterward He was hungry. Now when the tempter came to Him, he said, "If You are the Son of God, command that these stones become bread." But He answered and said, "It is written, 'Man shall not live by bread alone, but by every word that proceeds from the mouth of God.'" Then the devil took Him up into the holy city, set Him on the pinnacle of the temple, and said to Him, "If You are the Son of God, throw Yourself down. For it is written: 'He shall give His angels charge over you,' and, 'In their hands they shall bear you up, lest you dash your foot against a stone.'" Jesus said to him, "It is written again, 'You shall not tempt the LORD your God'" (Matthew 4:1-7).

There is none like Jesus in the whole earth; yet He, like us, was tested. It is interesting to see that the devil used the same type of temptations on Jesus that he uses on us this very day. But more than that, he tests, not when we are strong and energized, but rather, when we are at our lowest point in life. He does this so that he can have an advantage over us. It would be relatively easy to pass a test if we had proper exercise, a sumptuous dinner the night before, and a hearty breakfast on the morning of the test. What I am trying to say is that we wouldn't struggle as much if we knew beforehand exactly what was going to be on the test. We would attempt to prepare ourselves for it.

Unfortunately, we do not always have foreknowledge of those things. We are not always prepared mentally, emotionally, financially, or spiritually for the tests that life gives us without fair notice. Know this: Tests will come. They often come unannounced. Jesus, being at a physically low point having just completed a 40-day fast in the presence of His Father, is now being confronted with a serpentine problem.

That moment did not appear to be the best time to give a test. It almost seemed like the enemy had an unfair advantage over Jesus. Satan may have pondered, *If Jesus is at His lowest point, I can probably get Him to do anything that I ask.* Since Satan had only this opportunity, he wanted to take his best shot. His best shot, however, was not trying to convince Jesus to sin.

The devil was not so much trying to get Jesus to yield to a mundane temptation as he was trying to get Jesus to lose faith in what He already knew to be true. He fiendishly attempted to convince Jesus to lose faith in the Word. He wanted Jesus to forget the words and commission that His Father gave to Him. For Jesus, that ultimately meant that He would have to lose faith in Himself, for He is the Living Word.

Understand that Jesus' shed blood on the cross at Calvary takes full care of the sin issue. If you have yielded to temptation, quickly run to Jesus for forgiveness and receive your pardon. Although sin has its obvious dangers and consequences, faithlessness can be far more detrimental. Satan's greatest test toward us is not so much to get us to sin. He knows far more than many Christians do how potent the blood of Jesus is. He recognizes that if the children of God will tap into the flow, they will be instantly freed from their sin.

On the other hand, how can you be freed from faithlessness? The devil tries more than ever to get you to forget the promises that God has made to you in His Word. He tries to convince you that you are not who God says you are. Added to that, he tricks you into believing and accepting the lie that you cannot do what God has told you that you are fully capable of doing. After you have accepted all these lies from the devil as truth, you then begin to start seeing yourself the way the devil wants you to be viewed— defeated.

If he can accomplish this, then he has won. The test that Jesus passed was not merely a test of the lust of the eyes, the lust of the flesh, and the pride of life as so many scholars teach. Those tests were fundamental for Jesus. He would have easily passed those tests without even considering them. This test was one of faith. Would Jesus fall into the trap that so many believers fall into, some subconsciously and others quite consciously? Would Jesus maintain what His Father already told Him? Simply asked, "Would Jesus keep the faith?"

I believe you should ask yourself the same question. What point of lowness and depression does it take for you to change your mind about God's Word? Perhaps you may have been given strong prophetic words concerning greatness in your near future. You knew from the time you heard the words of prophecy that it was a word from God. It immediately connected in your soul. You had been praying to hear a word from the Lord to confirm what you thought were just mere speculations about your future. Bang! It happened.

You got your personal word from the Lord. As the word comes forth, you don't seem to have a problem receiving the word. It feels so right. But wait a minute. Now the word is over. And it's up to you to walk in the word, continue to believe the word, and nurture that word until it comes to full fruition. You've got to guard the word that God has placed in your heart. You have to make sure that the word that was sown is not easily uprooted. You have to keep the faith. Consider what Jesus said about this same topic:

> *A sower went out to sow his seed. And as he sowed, some fell by the wayside; and it was trampled down, and the birds of the air devoured it. Some fell on rock; and as soon as it sprang up, it withered away because it lacked moisture. And some fell among thorns, and the thorns sprang up with it and choked it. But others fell on good ground, sprang up, and yielded a crop a hundredfold...* (Luke 8:5-8).

It never ceases to amaze me how God will give a word to an individual that he or she will be a millionaire. Then that person winds up bouncing checks and getting even deeper into debt. That doesn't seem to make reasonable sense to the natural mind. Or you may have received a word from God that your cancer-filled body was going to

You are not exempt from being tested.

be healed in Jesus' name. When you visit the doctor, she informs you that you have at best three weeks to live. Why do things happen like this? Is God playing childish games with His children? Or do situations like these serve a greater purpose? Do they have a deeper meaning?

Maybe it is quite possible that God wants your situation to appear bleak to your eye so, when He turns it around, you know that it was completely a work of God, not man. Perhaps God enjoys working in situations where it seems like there is nothing to work with. Maybe God wants you to grasp the point that whatever other people have to say about you is totally unimportant. What God says is final. So if God says you're ahead, you're on top, you are rich, you are healed, you are saved and delivered, and you have everything you need— it is so! However, once you get the good word, realize that the word will be tried.

The major point that I am making is that you are not exempt from being tested. Faith that isn't tested isn't faith at all. Every biblical character who played an important role was tested. People listed in Hebrews' hall of faith made it there only because they passed the faith test. For example, God told Abraham that his barren and old wife Sarah would bear a son and that he, Abraham, would be the father of many nations. That was his test.

Joseph endured multiple tests. First, after receiving a dream in which he was shown to rule over his family, his brothers conspired against him and sold him into slavery. Then, while in his master's house, he endured false accusation from Potiphar's wife and was thrown in jail, an innocent man.

The early believers, who left everything to follow the Lord Jesus Christ, their Savior, knew that the spiritual benefits would be great. What they didn't realize, perhaps, was the cost involved—persecution and trouble wherever they went. The devout Jews who had converted to Christianity were targeted far more than Gentiles since the practicing Jews considered Jesus and all that He stood for as a threat to their organized religion and rich tradition.

They (the New Testament believers) were a marked people. Crazy neurotics like Saul of Tarsus literally murdered people who identified with Jesus. He made it his job and passion to torment the saints. The new believers started by confessing their unfailing commitment and faith in Jesus Christ, then endured the test.

Let us not forget Jesus. Jesus promised His Father that He would do whatever it took to redeem fallen humanity back to a proper relationship with God. He knew that the end result of His efforts would be life and redemption from destruction for God's children rather than death. When the news quickly began to spread that the Messiah had come, He did not receive the usual fanfare associated with a kingly order. The people hated Him. It was a test.

> *He is despised and rejected by men, a Man of sorrows and acquainted with grief. And we hid, as it were, our faces from Him; He was despised, and we did not esteem Him. Surely He has borne our griefs and carried our sorrows; yet we esteemed Him stricken, smitten by God, and afflicted* (Isaiah 53:3-4).

You see, no matter who you are, life is going to try your faith. Your faith *will* be tested. When your faith is tested, you become refined in the process. You begin to reflect a clearer image of Jesus Christ. We, like Him, need our faith to be tested. It validates whether our convictions are pure or not. It proves that our testimony is real. Passing our test process makes us eligible to speak into the lives of others.

After all, it is hard to convince another person of something if you have never experienced it. Your words have a lot more authority when you can say, "You can make it, you can come out victorious because I've gone through it, too, and I know."

> *Behold, I have refined you, but not as silver; I have tested you in the furnace of affliction. For My own*

sake, for My own sake, I will do it; for how should My name be profaned? And I will not give My glory to another (Isaiah 48:10-11).

Chapter Six

The Talk of Faith and the Walk of Faith

Talking the Talk

*For assuredly, I say to you, whoever **says** to this mountain, "Be removed and be cast into the sea," and does not doubt in his heart, but believes that those things he **says** will be done, he will have **whatever he says*** (Mark 11:23).

But what does it say? "The word is near you, in your mouth and in your heart" (that is, the word of faith which we preach) (Romans 10:8).

The rich in faith talk a certain way. When life deals a raw blow to people whose faith is weak, they tend to talk despairingly. Those whose faith is strong, however, usually view such a turn as an opportunity through which God will bless them. For instance, suppose a believer gets laid off from his or her job. Typically people assume their lives are about to take a downward turn.

Because they looked to their jobs as their sole source of provision, they become devastated when their employer makes the decision that their services are no longer needed. They may choose to stop paying all their bills and expenses just in case they need the money for things like food and clothing. They start to speak words of financial decrease. "How I am going to pay my bills? I am going to lose everything I worked so hard to get. It would probably make sense for me to just go ahead and turn the car in; I'm sure I won't be able to make the payments. We'll have to take the kids out of private school; we'll never be able to afford the tuition. Maybe we should move into a smaller place—there is far too much expense associated with this place." The negative list of possible fear talk could go on forever. Hopefully, you are getting the point.

Faith people talk a totally different language. Suppose you get around people who don't speak your language while you don't speak their language. You won't understand them, and neither will they understand you. Why? It's simple. You don't know how to speak the language, nor do you understand it when it is spoken. That is why people who are faithless become so confused when people of faith start talking that "faith talk."

They don't understand the language and become frustrated since they cannot communicate effectively.

When faith-filled people get laid off from their jobs, they begin to rejoice. They say things like, "I thank You, Lord, for giving me the opportunity to advance. God is setting me up for a promotion. I'm getting ready to earn more than I ever have in my entire life. Perhaps I should go and find someone to be a blessing to because God's been so good to me. I am so excited and wait with great anticipation for what God has in store for me. Praise God!"

It is your heart and verbal response that ultimately determine your outcome in life's tough situations.

You must understand that for an unbeliever or a weak-minded Christian, that kind of talk simply sounds foolish. Unbelievers act on feelings and senses while faith-filled believers respond only in faith. I believe that it is your heart and verbal response that ultimately determine your outcome in life's tough situations. You can actually speak negative things into existence if you continually voice them. In the same manner, you can speak God's desires and make them a reality in your life if you understand how powerful your tongue actually is.

We faith-filled believers speak what we know God desires for us in any given situation. Because of that we never see defeat. You might say, "That's silly and unrealistic. If you're sick, you're sick. If you're laid off, you're just laid off. If the doctor diagnosed you with an incurable disease, then you're just going to die. It's simply your fate." That is not how faith-filled believers think. We believe that we can look at a situation that seems to be dead and speak life into it.

> Therefore it is of faith that it might be according to grace, so that the promise might be sure to all the seed, not only to those who are of the law, but also to those who are of the faith of Abraham, who is the father of us all (as it is written, "I have made you a father of many nations") in the presence of Him whom he believed—God, who gives life to the dead and **calls those things which do not exist as though they did**; who, contrary to hope, in hope believed, so that he became the father of many nations, according to what was spoken, "So shall your descendants be" (Romans 4:16-18).

Because we are the seed of Abraham we call those things that do not exist as though they did. That's how we can call a marriage, on the brink of divorce, a great model marriage. We can call a body, racked with pain from cancer that has metastasized, a totally healthy body. Often believers will call themselves rich although they may have a significant amount of debt yet to pay off. We only do this because God's Word tells us that when we do, we (by faith) can change an evil order.

So you must be certain not to give your tongue to the enemy by saying those things that already exist. God has given you the power to create a life of righteousness and joy in the Holy Ghost with your tongue, or a life of defeat where you feel like dying. How you choose to talk, what words you choose to speak on a continual basis, is not up to God. It's up to you.

Just know that the words you choose, the talk you talk, really does have a life-changing impact on your situation. It worked for me when I conquered cancer through faith in the name of Jesus. Since God is no respecter of persons, I am sure that it will work for you, too.

Death and life are in the power of the tongue, and those who love it will eat its fruit (Proverbs 18:21).

The Walk of Faith

For we walk by faith, not by sight (2 Corinthians 5:7).

If you have made it this far in the book, then I believe you just might have what it takes to be a person of impeccable faith. By now you probably have realized that faith is a walk, or in other words, it is a lifestyle. That means you exercise your faith continually. Doing it once or twice does not mean you are living by faith. It simply doesn't work like that.

If you want faith to work for you all the time, then you must live it all the time. Faith must become your lifestyle. Let me say it another way: Faith must become habitual. Just like you perform personal hygiene each day without being told, you need to walk in faith every day.

Faith must become habitual. Think about it. You probably don't have to be reminded to show up at your job. If you have worked at your job on a pretty consistent basis, then the habit of just showing up has become a common part of your life.

You don't try to brush your teeth; you just do. You don't forcefully show up at work; you just make it there each day. Why? You have done it so many times, to do otherwise would feel most abnormal to you. In the same way, living a lifestyle of faith should become like a second nature. Until you reach that point, though, you will always be working in the flesh realm to make things come to pass. Eventually all your fleshly working and striving will make you miserable.

You have to make the decision that you will allow God to be your everything. You have to trust Him without reservation. It's when you get to that point that you will really be walking by faith. Then it's no longer you, but Christ inside you, who is getting the job done. As with anything, in the beginning stages you've got to *practice* trusting God.

Unfortunately, we live in a world that is plagued with such wickedness and anti-godliness traits that trusting

God has become a mocked thing to do. As a result, we have learned bad behavior that has obviously produced bad fruit. Now we all must be retrained in our minds and spirits to think as God thinks. As you begin to walk by faith and believe God for everything in your life, your faith will strengthen more and more. In time, walking by faith will become as natural to you as swimming is to a fish or flying is to a bird of the air.

When you reach the place where faith is a natural part of your life, you will really be walking the walk of faith. You, like the patriarchs of old, will be setting new faith records and doing mighty exploits in the name of the Lord. It is also at this place where you will live on such a high plane that going in reverse will not be an option for you ever again. Your faith will continue to develop and grow strong. At some point—and that time will be soon—God Himself will brag about you to Satan, informing him that you, like Job, possess faith that will stand the tests of time—*faith that takes a lickin'!*

Chapter Seven

Persistent Faith

And you will be hated by all for My name's sake. But he who endures to the end will be saved (Matthew 10:22).

Of all the qualities a person could have, I believe that the quality of persistence is one of the greatest. To continue in the face of great danger or when it looks like your situation is utterly hopeless is unusually merit worthy. For most folks, faith is more of a spontaneous emotional response than a commitment to never quit. More people are ready to "join up" in the "walk by faith" club if they can be guaranteed instant gratification and immediate results. Few, however, stick and stay in it for the long haul when they discover that they may have to work to obtain the prize.

I've always had a knack for business and business ventures. I've sold everything from cars to houses to accessories for women to men's clothing. Over the years I have noticed how people automatically think of me when they get ready to go into a new business venture as one of their potential clients. Most people who know me know that I sincerely love to help people to prosper and get ahead in life. For the most part, I do whatever I can to be a blessing to individuals who show me by their example that they are committed to what they are in.

So over the years I've gotten involved with several different network-marketing ventures because people whom I dearly love or whom I really respect asked me to get involved. I can honestly admit that I never got involved with these businesses because of the money. I'm a much wiser businessman than that. From experience I have come to recognize that, in order to create wealth, you have to be totally committed to whatever wealth-building engine you choose to use.

You can't start with this business today, then by next month go on to an entirely different project. Before the year is over you've jumped to another three or four businesses. When people behave like this, they send a strong message to me. They are telling me two major things through their actions. The first and more obvious message that I am getting is that investing in them is a bad choice and that my money would be better invested elsewhere.

The second message that I receive from their actions is that they really don't have the level of persistent faith that is needed in order to build a strong business. Most strong businesses, whether network marketing or the more traditional conventional forms of corporate business building, usually take anywhere from five to seven years to establish a real strong foundation. Anything less than that won't develop the character needed to maintain real financial success.

Unfortunately, most people don't think like that. Most folks wimp out. They give up before the real fight has even begun. Another example of a lack of persistence can been seen in many pastors in our country. A large number of pastors who either begin their own ministries or are placed within a ministry quit within their first two years. According to the National Prayer News Service, "33 percent of pastors leave churches due to conflicts with the congregation and unclear goals or expectations. The average tenure of associate ministers and staff is less than two years. An estimated 25 percent of all pastors relocate every year."[1]

The first day of the pastorate may appear to be peaches and cream. The real battle comes later on down the road, after the church members have gotten the chance to know you, evaluate you, criticize you, and then give you a failing grade. Somehow the enemy convinces many pastors that persisting is simply not worth it. Based on these conditions it's not very hard to see why so many choose the road they do. After all, most pastors I know are gifted in various areas and could probably do very well in a totally different profession. That being the case, why should they persist? Read on.

This attitude is the very reason churches fail. It's why ministries fall and never get up. This same reasoning or train of thought explains why businesses resort to scandalous corporate crime, not caring about the trusting investors who are left defrauded in the process. Sixty percent of marriages fail. Why is there so much failure? Why don't they all simply just get back into the fight? It is because most people refuse to activate the quality of persistence that lies dormant within most of us. To wake it up we must simply believe. We must believe that, although we have been knocked down, the fight ain't over. It's as simple as that.

Knocked Down But Not Knocked Out

I'm a fan of boxing. Of course the most famous of boxing greats is the one and only Muhammad Ali. Numerous books have been written about his life and boxing career, but here are a few facts:

- Out of 61 matches, he won 56 and lost 5.

- Out of 56 wins, 37 were knockouts.

- In 1960 Ali was the Olympic Light Heavyweight Gold Medalist and three-time heavyweight champion of the world.

Muhammad Ali also was known to be somewhat mouthy. He said "I fly like a butterfly and sting like a bee" so often that it became his conviction. He began to believe that he could not lose.

In 1970, in "the fight of the century," Muhammad Ali faced Joe Frazier at Madison Square Garden. Not only was it the first time he lost a professional fight, but he also was knocked down to the canvas. Still, Ali got back up and fought to the end. He lost the fight, yes, but he did not lose his career, his faithful fans, or the legacy he had worked so hard to establish. Persistence was the key to his success. No matter how many times life knocks you down, you can get back up again. That's *faith that takes a lickin'.*

Later Muhammad Ali lost to Trevor Berbick in the Bahamas. Not long after that loss, Ali told the world that he would no longer fight professionally. Think about that for a minute. Did he resign? Did he really give up? Was his career of fighting actually over? I don't think so. Even today Ali is remembered as the greatest athlete of the past century. His name has become commonplace to everyone in civilized society, not just with sport lovers.

Although he technically lost his last fight, he is still winning many victories. His spirit of persistence can still be clearly seen on television commercials, billboard advertisements, and autographed boxing paraphernalia. Now Ali gets paid big bucks for his advice and often as a sports commentator. He's fighting a different fight now, and he's still winning. Why? He possesses an attitude that every believer needs desperately. That attitude is persistence.

Whatever you do, don't give the world what they want. Remember that they want you to fail. They expect you to give in at the first sign of pressure. Don't let the negative comments that your past acquaintances spewed over you actually count for anything. Don't allow the images of failure that your family and friends had of you hold true. It is God who has already predetermined your expected end. And that end is a great one! You have got to draw from the well within you and literally force persistence out of you, especially when the enemy tries to convince you that it's all over.

You lost. So what? You made some horrible mistakes. So what? Your business was in the red last quarter and you owe millions to your creditors. So what? Maybe your church members walked out and left you all alone with no one to lead. *It's still not over.* There's a whole lot more people waiting to hear God's Word. Go after them. Maybe your spouse told you that he or she never wanted to see you again. Your marriage is not over unless you decide that it's over. No matter what your problem is, choose to persist through it. God promises that you will come out on top. Your faith will soon prove that you are a winner!

You made men ride over our heads; we went through fire and through water, yet You brought us out into a place of abundance (Psalm 66:12 NAS).

Persistence—A Kingdom Quality

"If at first you don't succeed, try, try again."

—William Edward Hickson (1803–1870)

British Educator

"Never say die."

—Ancient Proverb

Persistence has many valuable rewards in the natural realm. But did you know that persistence is a quality of the kingdom of God? It's one of the traits that make us very much like our Creator. God Himself possesses a "never quit" attitude about Him. More than that, He always gets what He desires, regardless of the price. If we are going to be like God, then we must embrace the reality that giving up is just not an option.

The primary and focal message of Jesus Christ was, and still is, the gospel of the kingdom. The whole idea behind this gospel of the kingdom is that the King, the Lord Jesus Christ, reigns and rules in this earth realm through His children. If He cannot be Lord and King through His children on this earth, then His power and His dominion can never be seen. In reality, God becomes powerless. Doesn't that sound somewhat strange? How can God, Creator of heaven and earth, become powerless?

It's as simple as this. When God cannot use you as a vessel to transmit His power and wondrous works through, He becomes powerless because He has no other method of displaying His power and might. God does not have any other options. Just face it: God's tagged you and now you're it. For centuries, God has been patiently waiting for someone to just believe that the impossible is truly possible. And even if the impossible does not happen for you right away, He expects that you will persist until it does. That is the kind of faith that God is continually seeking.

God is continually seeking people with persistent faith.

There are many examples in the Scriptures of people who displayed this kingdom quality of persistence. Paul the apostle is just one of many who portrayed such character. During his missions trip to Corinth, the apostle Paul spent all his time preaching and teaching about Jesus Christ the Messiah. He never missed Sabbath worship at the synagogues, for he knew that the weekly in-gathering of the Jewish people was a great opportunity to witness to them about Jesus.

Sadly, the Jews living in Corinth opposed Paul and his teachings about Jesus Christ. It became increasingly harder for Paul to continue preaching to the Jewish people. As a result, Paul decided that he would no longer try

118

to reach a hard-hearing people. Instead, he would focus on pouring out his life preaching and teaching about Jesus Christ to the Gentiles.

Paul, perhaps wondering in himself if he should even bother anymore, concluded that Corinth was probably not worth the time invested in exchange for such a small return. With that, he set his eyes on different regions. He wanted to go to places where his message would be appreciated and more readily accepted. His vision was becoming increasingly obscured because of the people's negative behavior. Just before he quit, God spoke to him in a vision. God gave Paul renewed sight. Prior to this the apostle had focused only on the negative people in Corinth. But after this vision, he became more focused on the potential new converts that would be changed by his message.

> *One night the Lord spoke to Paul in a vision and told him, "Don't be afraid! Speak out! Don't quit! For I am with you and no one can harm you. Many people here in this city belong to me." So Paul stayed there the next year and a half, teaching the truths of God* (Acts 18:9-11 TLB).

The Living Bible says that God told Paul not to quit. God was trying to tell Paul to persist, not give up, stick it out. The blessing and reward would come if he persisted. It would have been a major loss to the kingdom of God if Paul had left this place. There were thousands of hungry hearts waiting to hear about Jesus. However, if he had allowed negative people to discourage him, he would never have reached the people who were ready to hear the Gospel.

There is a message in this story: Stay away from negative people. Negative people have a poisonous liquid upon them. Once they touch you with this poisonous matter, you'll get infected with their virus of quitting. Paul stayed in the city for one and a half more years. He had great meetings and many people were made disciples of Christ. Had he quit, many people would have been lost and the blood of all their souls would have been placed on Paul's shoulders.

There is so much wisdom in older ministers who have been in kingdom work for decades upon decades. I love to listen to their stories—particularly those who survived attack and criticism. I find that it inspires me when I hear how they persevered despite the lack of support from Christians. Often without enough funds or support, these pioneers of the early 20th century outlasted the lies and scandals thrown against them.

How did they make it? Some of these ministers told me they felt like it was all hell against them. Nevertheless, they made it. They "kept the faith." As a result, not only did they minister to and bring healing to thousands of people, but they also can look forward to a crown of life. How blessed it is to live a kingdom life! And that means having the trait of persistence.

I have fought the good fight, I have finished the race, I have kept the faith. Finally, there is laid up for me the crown of righteousness, which the Lord, the righteous Judge, will give to me on that Day, and not to me only but also to all who have loved His appearing (2 Timothy 4:7-8).

You have a great responsibility given to you. The important thing to realize is that it's not about you. It's not about how you feel or your personal emotions. What God has placed in your hands is for the betterment of all humanity. If you quit, then people will inevitably suffer. The price of such neglect is a price that I am not willing to pay. We must persist.

I believe that the ultimate example of God's persistence can be seen in His unceasing commitment to redeem fallen humanity. Just thinking about His persistence to deliver us causes me to become a bit emotional. First, we (humanity) were at fault. It was through Adam's sin that we all inherited the curse of the law. *"Therefore, just as through one man sin entered the world, and death through sin, and thus death spread to all men, because all sinned"* (Romans 5:12). It's clear to see that we are the ones who started off in the wrong. Even though we were wrong, God loved us so dearly that He made it His mission to position us back in a proper relationship with Him again.

All the money in the world combined could not pay the price for one man's sin, let alone the sins of the entire world. So God had to originate a plan, one that would achieve a high cause. He had to create a plan to restore man back to his rightful place with God in covenant fellowship. Since there were no resources sufficient enough to pay this great debt, only a human sacrifice would suffice.

This sacrifice could not be just any sacrifice, though. It could not have been you or me; it had to be someone who was just like God, someone who literally came from God's loins. What better one than God's only Son? God was so persistent that He took matters into His own hands and gave His only begotten Son. He did it to prove to us how much we are actually worth to Him. If God can be so persistent as to allow His only Son to be sacrificed on a cross, how about you? Where do you stand? To what extreme will you go to establish your convictions? God is looking for someone with persistent faith. He is building an army of faith-filled believers. Will you enlist?

For God so loved the world that He gave His only begotten Son, that whoever believes in Him should not perish but have everlasting life. For God did not send His Son into the world to condemn the world, but that the world through Him might be saved (John 3:16-17).

The Spirit "Essence" of a Winner

What makes some people winners and so many others losers? What is the actual component that makes people continue to fight even when they are tired and worn out? I believe that there lies in each and every person a God-given spirit that, once tapped into, will birth the winner within. Winning in life is a spiritual thing. It's not simply something that you do from time to time. Winning is who you are. It is what you become particularly when life has dealt to you a hard blow. Winning is what you are made of.

Have you ever watched a professional team sport on television or in person? Since I live in Texas, which is Dallas Cowboy country, I have had the good fortune of watching a winning team nearly all my life. I can be a little bit biased about NFL teams. Surely you can appreciate that. If you are not a Cowboys fan, don't get offended. If you can't beat 'em, just join 'em.

The point I want to make is that, when opposing teams are competing to win the game, both teams are eagerly fighting with all they have inside them to win the game. It's obvious that, whether it's a preseason game or a regular season game or even the playoffs, either team is bound to lose. Somebody's got to be the winner and, of course, someone's got to be the loser. I've seen the Cowboys fight hard to win a game. For some unknown reason they just could not pull it off. After they lost a game, where did that put them?

Were they condemned to becoming losers forever? Would they be barred from ever having a chance at winning another Super Bowl? Were they banned from the

NFL? Do you think that the owner of the team would sell the franchise because they lost so miserably? Of course all these questions seem a bit silly. They seem silly because of the undeniable spirit that you and I know exists in most professional teams.

You have the essence of a winner. Winning is who you are.

Each loss only creates more of an appetite within them to make them want to win the next time around. This is the kind of spirit that creates winners out of those who may have lost a few rounds in life. This spirit says, "No matter what I've been through, I am obligated to myself and to my God to get up and try again." That's the spirit that I am talking about.

It's that still small voice that tells you to keep on moving although every thing outside of you screams, "GIVE UP!" You just can't seem to give up even when you want to. Sometimes it seems unfair. Why is it that you are so marked? Why can't you give up like other people can? You have the essence of a winner. That essence is not determined by how many wins you achieve in life.

You may not have had that many wins at all. In fact, you may have a long record of losses. The essence of being a winner comes on the person who will fight one more time, try again and again, and keep moving forward, even though everything in view looks like it's not going to work out. That's the spirit that I'm talking about.

I believe that you have this spirit. The simple fact that you are reading this book makes you different than more than 70 percent of the population.

If you have been born again, there's a spirit on you, an essence that defines your character. You can't shake it off; neither can you wash it off. It has become a part of who you are. It is the spirit of Christ in you. Jesus was beat down and killed. Everybody seemed to think that He was a goner, never to be seen anymore. But He possessed this spirit that I am talking about. He could not stay down. He had to get up. And so do you.

> *And since we have the same spirit of faith, according to what is written, "I believed and therefore I spoke," we also believe and therefore speak, knowing that He who raised up the Lord Jesus will also raise us up with Jesus, and will present us with you* (2 Corinthians 4:13-14).

Running the Race

> *Whatever your hand finds to do, do it with your might; for there is no work or device or knowledge or wisdom in the grave where you are going. I returned and saw under the sun that—The race is not to the swift, nor the battle to the strong, nor bread to the wise, nor riches to men of understanding, nor favor to men of skill; but time and chance happen to them all* (Ecclesiastes 9:10-11).

Pastor Aaron D. Lewis is a longtime dear friend of mine from Connecticut. Years ago, when we ministered at different events for each other, we used to go out to restaurants and eat and fellowship over great food. Now, Aaron was a good-sized, mid-height man who liked barbeque and mesquite chicken and beef ribs. In fact, every time he came to Texas to visit me or preach, we'd go out, at his request, to this local restaurant that served the best beef ribs and chicken. It was like a tradition for us.

Eventually we spent less time together as our schedules each got busier and busier. Oh, we still stayed in touch by phone, but we didn't see each other for two or more years. So the next time I saw him, I was shocked. Aaron was about 50 pounds lighter, and frankly, I thought he looked too skinny.

As we were about to head out the door to go to a restaurant—me thinking we'd be going to our traditional place for ribs and chicken—I asked him what he wanted. To my surprise, he replied that he'd like some "vegetables, fruits, and pasta." I thought he was joking until he explained that he had started running marathons and had totally changed the way he ate. Now he ate foods that would help him have endurance and run, so that he could finish the race.

I listened as he told me how there were some foods that could give him greater endurance. Others would totally sabotage his efforts to race. Since he wanted to

run and finish—and for the good of his overall health—
he chose to train his mind to accept new foods and avoid
other foods that he used to love.

The point is, my friend made a conscious choice to
change in order to finish his race. How about you? What
choices are you making today that will affect your spirit
of endurance tomorrow? How can you know for sure that
you will last once you have entered your next race in the
kingdom? Are you feeding from doubt, disbelief, and the
negative limiting opinions of other? If you are, then you
are feeding off of the wrong stuff.

Eventually your spiritual body and your spirit to win
will shut down. The reason is that you have not been
properly prepared to run the faith race. In this race it is
imperative to guard what comes into your ear. It is your
ear that is the entry gate to your spirit. Just like my
friend made a conscious choice to alter what he eats in
order to improve his performance, you, too, need to
change what you have become accustomed to. You have
to become conditioned to finishing your race and doing
whatever it takes to accomplish that goal.

You have to realize ahead of time that the permanent
benefits are far greater than the pain of adapting to better habits. Knowing that will help you to get through. You
have to change your thoughts and reprogram your mind.
Start thinking on things that will add miles to your stride.
Start confessing and meditating on the Word of God to

ensure your success and to add fuel to your faith. You ask, "Brother Coe, I am not sure what to think on. Do you have any suggestions?" I am glad you asked. If you promise to commit to the list that I am going to suggest to you, I'll guarantee you that you will develop persistent faith. This list is in Philippians 4:8:

> *Finally, brethren, whatever things are true, whatever things are noble, whatever things are just, whatever things are pure, whatever things are lovely, whatever things are of good report, if there is any virtue and if there is anything praiseworthy— meditate on these things.*

Chapter Eight

Violent Faith

Taking Back Stolen Property...By Force

And from the days of John the Baptist until now the kingdom of heaven suffers violence, and the violent take it by force (Matthew 11:12).

There is an element of the faith life that many people fail to recognize. This element of faith is not only necessary in general, but also necessary specifically for obtaining stolen promises. We can label it as forceful faith. There are some things in life that will come simply because it's your inheritance. Other things will come to you in life because you worked hard for it; you earned it. Many other things you will acquire because you operate on a basic sort of "entry level" faith. However, some things will only come to you when, by faith, you forcefully take them.

Of all the categories that I mentioned, this category of taking something by force has to be the most challenging, yet the most rewarding. The things that you take by force are usually things of great and irreplaceable value. I've heard ministers coach their congregations about going into the enemy's camp and taking back what the devil has stolen from them. They get all psyched up. Sad to say, not only do they *not* receive what they went to claim, but the devil also nearly beats them to death. Why? They don't understand spiritual warfare as it relates to faith.

You have to understand some things about spiritual warfare, fervent prayer, and obedience before you dare invade the enemy's camp. Sure, the devil has your stuff. That's true. However, your stuff is in *his* camp. That's the problem. You can't get your stuff unless you take it by force. More importantly, you can't take it back unless you have a strategy for doing so! Another thing you must realize, which some ministers don't know themselves, is that the stuff you are going to take back on this level is not usually material things.

On this level, the stuff that you take back are usually things that money cannot buy. For example, if your car was repossessed, you really don't need to go into the enemy's camp to get back your car. It was your own ignorance that caused you to lose it in the first place. So you've got to understand that the devil didn't take your car. The "repo" guy took it, with justifiable reasoning.

130

You did not pay for it. Not paying your car note is almost like stealing a car.

It you pay your note you'll keep your car, no questions asked. So the devil is not usually after things that your money can buy. But wisdom, prudence, understanding, and proper management will get you anything in this life that you desire. Those virtues can get you anything from a Fortune 500 business to a jet airplane to the house of your dreams to a Harvard medical degree.

The enemy is not after your house or car; he is after your marriage and children.

Even those things are not what the enemy treasures most. Instead, he wants things that are invaluable—your children, your solid relationships, your marriage and family structure. He wants your future. He is after your destiny. He is determined to claim these things at any cost. It is these things that he literally lusts after. And it is these things that we must guard with all diligence when we have them. Once they are in his possession, we'll have to fight tooth and nail to get them back.

So understand that you don't have to forcefully take back your car or house. You can get those at any time if you choose to do what it takes in the natural. Discipline will get you those things. But your son or daughter who has been stolen from your control and is now on drugs, involved in criminal activities, or serving time in jail is under Satan's control. And quite honestly, he has no plans on giving that child back to you. Hence, you're going have to take your family back by force and acquire the needed knowledge to successfully do so.

They Belong to You

One of the things that will help you get back what the devil has stolen from you is knowing in your heart of hearts that what you actually have a claim on is what you are going after. Why is that important? If you don't have a right to something, then you cannot use legal force to reclaim it. For example, you may have left your keys in a running car and some idiot decides to steal it. What do you do? What is your response to the theft? Automatically you know to call the local police and report the incident.

When you call the police they will ask you a series of questions pertaining to the car. What make is the car? What is the model of the car? What year was the car built? What color is your vehicle? Would you happen to know the Vehicle Identification Number (VIN)? They ask questions more about the features of the car than anything else. Usually they won't ask you if you own the car. That's a given. They automatically assume that you own the car. You have a title that proves it.

Far too often, believers waste their time seizing property that doesn't belong to them. Some believers spend time fighting fights that are not their fights to begin with. And in the process they discover that the enemy has won. He does not win simply because he still has your stuff. He wins because you've wasted so much time on nothing. *You must have a claim on what you are going after.* In that same time period you could have gained far more than you lost. So there are times when you have to assess your fights and decide up front whether the fight is worth it. More than that, you have to predetermine if it's your fight at all or if it really belongs to the Lord.

Suppose you went to the store and bought a jar of mayonnaise. The jar of mayonnaise cost approximately $3.29. You had a 20-cent coupon that you forgot to give the cashier. You discover the forgotten coupon when you are about 20 miles away from the supermarket and nearly 2 miles from your home. You've got a choice to make. You can turn around and drive back 20 miles and reclaim your 20 cents. After all, it does belong to you.

Another choice that you could make is to forget about it altogether, seeing that if you go back you'll spend 20 times more in automobile fuel than what you would have received in the coupon savings. It rightfully belongs to you, but is it worth it? You have a rightful claim on it, but is it really worth it? If it's not, then go on to achieve bigger and better things. However, if it is worth it, then fight until you die to get back your child, your spouse, your spiritual walk, your pastor, and so on. Hopefully you are getting the point. If you have a title to it, and it has an appreciating value, then you need to go for it.

Sounding the Alarm

If you plan on getting back stolen goods, even if you are a pretty passive person, then you are going to have to make some noise. I don't want you to make noise simply for the sake of making noise. That'll get you nowhere. No, when you sound the alarm, you are making a declaration to the enemy that you are fully prepared to conquer him and reclaim all your goods. The sound that will be heard is a sound of war. Now here's the God part—not the good part, but the God part. You make the sound of war, but God actually fights your battle.

You make the sound of war, but God actually fights your battle.

Of course, God doesn't physically fight any battle for you. He can't, simply because He is not confined or defined by the physical world. He is not physical, so He cannot fight physical fights. Physical fights are for you to battle out, not God. God uses spiritual power to conquer spiritual problems. That's the strategy God uses. His strategies are often completely opposite of what we would have thought of. They usually don't make sense to our thinking. A clear

134

example of this can be seen in how Gideon defeated an entire army, never having had any military training or skill.

God used Gideon, a wheat farmer, to defeat the formidable army of the Midianites. This army far exceeded the number of men that Gideon's army had. They were more skilled in weaponry and assassination. When God told him to form an army, Gideon started out with 32,000 people in his army. That seems like a large number, but the Midian soldiers still far outnumbered the Israelite army. Then God decided to use a series of character tests to further reduce Gideon's army from 32,000 men to a mere and measly 300. This is a strategy that only God would choose. Our minds would tell us that the more people in our army, the better chance we have of winning. However, that's not how God thinks.

> When Gideon heard the dream and its interpretation, he worshiped God. He returned to the camp of Israel and called out, "Get up! The LORD has given the Midianite camp into your hands." Dividing the three hundred men into three companies, he placed trumpets and empty jars in the hands of all of them, with torches inside. "Watch me," he told them. "Follow my lead. When I get to the edge of the camp, do exactly as I do. When I and all who are with me blow our trumpets, then from all around the camp blow yours and shout, 'For the LORD and for Gideon'"

> (Judges 7:15-18 NIV).

When the three hundred trumpets sounded, the LORD caused the men throughout the camp to turn on each other with their swords. The army fled to Beth Shittah toward Zererah as far as the border of Abel Meholah near Tabbath

(Judges 7:22 NIV).

According to the Scriptures, God told Gideon to sound an alarm with trumpets and pitchers with lamps inside them. That doesn't seem much like even a guerrilla warfare approach. However, because of Gideon's obedience to employ this strange tactic that God ordered, the Israelites won the victory. The Bible says that, when they made the noise by sounding their alarm and breaking the pitchers, the enemy assumed that there were perhaps millions of soldiers on Gideon's side. They saw what appeared to them as a light show full of explosives and bombs. The fear of this sight and sound drove them into such hysteria that they began to kill one another. Sounding such an alarm is a tactic that I believe all faith-filled people should use.

Don't focus on using your own energy or strength. Use the strength of God. When your enemy is confused, he will become so afraid that he'll be forced to self-destruct—giving you free reign to go into his territory and safely take back your possession. However, in order to forcefully take back your stuff, you've got to first have a "whatever it takes" attitude. You have got to bind the strong man or simply get rid of him. As long as he has mobility, he can kill you. (Keep in mind I'm talking about the devil here, not people!)

Next, realize that, with every step you take, you must give total obedience to God. There is no compromise in this area. Finally, use God's power and not your own. For example, I have a cellular phone that at times gets on my last nerve, especially when I am talking to someone about something very important and the battery dies during the middle of my conversation. I've got to recharge the battery for several hours before it has a full charge and is ready to be used again. There are so many important deals that I could lose within that time. God's not like that. His power never runs out. So if you tap into His power, you'll never have to drain yours. That's a winning warfare strategy!

Common Misunderstandings About Faith

Many misconceptions about faith exist in people's minds. On top of that, a whole lot of false teaching is going around concerning this important issue of faith. For the most part, many people are just downright confused about faith. Unfortunately, some well-known preachers don't know God very well and, therefore, do not know how to walk by faith.

When I say this, I am not being critical of ministers. I have many areas in my own life for which I ask God to help me improve on every day. All I am saying is that, if someone teaches you a lesson you need to learn and he or she teaches it the wrong way, you will always be forced to follow that person's wrong pattern of teaching simply because you don't have the truth to compare it to. If you never knew the basic laws of addition and I told you that two plus two equals three or three plus four equals ten, you'd believe it.

You wouldn't believe it because you were stupid. Intelligence is not the issue. The only reason you would be so willing to believe it is because you don't know any better. You really don't know anything other than what was taught to you. So you need to have something to which you can compare what you've been taught. If I were to list all the wrong teachings concerning faith, this book could not contain all of my commentary on each item. So I've listed only five of what I believe are the more common misunderstandings about living a lifestyle of faith. I'll elaborate a bit on each point on this "hit list" to give you some clearer understanding on this vital subject of faith.

The "Hit List" of Misunderstandings About Faith

1. Faith is the absence of fear.

2. Faith is rewarded immediately—the microwave mentality.

3. We are always capable of judging faith in others.

4. The words I say don't really amount to much as it relates to my faith.

5. Whatever God's going to do, He is going to do. My faith won't make any difference at all.

Faith Is the Absence of Fear

So many preachers and teachers tell people that faith is the absence of fear. That is not true. Instead, faith is the courage to rise up and conquer your fear. Some people may try to act like they are not afraid of an angry pit bull dog frothing at the mouth, of an out-of-control wild animal, or of a crazy, illogical person pointing a gun directly at them. They may say that they walk in such a great level of faith that nothing ever scares them. As strong as that may sound, I'm not so sure that it's really the truth. Having faith does not mean that you aren't going to have times when you sense a little bit of fear.

The real issue is that you don't allow the seed of fear to grow within you. That is faith in action. When you have fear, that is your signal or cue that the spirit of faith needs to rise up inside you and defeat the spirit of fear that is trying so hard to plague you. You cannot conquer your fears by denying that they exist. Merely saying that you are not afraid is not going to remove your fears. Denial won't get you far in life, especially a life of faith. Just because you act like it's not there does not mean that it's not.

So what do you do? You have to become a replacement expert. What do I mean by this, you ask? You have to replace your fears with God's Word. This works quite well in any area where God's Word specifically addresses your present problem or condition. For example, when the doctor told me that I had colon cancer

Faith in action is when you don't allow the seed of fear to grow in you.

and would die from it, I can truthfully tell you that I was concerned. I didn't, however, let that concern consume me. If I had, I believe that I would probably be dead today.

Instead, I reminded myself of the Word of God concerning sickness and disease. You should make it a point to commit God's Word to memory. It will come in handy if you live long enough. David said, *"Thy word have I hid in mine heart, that I might not sin against thee"* (Psalm 119:11 KJV). It's the Word in your heart that you will have to draw from for strength and sustenance in your day of adversity. That's why reading God's Word is crucial. You can only act on what you know.

So when the doctor gave me this diagnosis, which promoted fear within me, I immediately replaced his word of fear and death with God's Word: *"But He was wounded for our transgressions, He was bruised for our iniquities; the chastisement for our peace was upon Him, and by His stripes we are healed"* (Isaiah 53:5). I started quoting this scripture until it became so real to me that nothing in the world could make me believe otherwise.

What I did is literally replace my fear with faith in what God's Word said. In time the sickness had to go because the faith was so powerful that, not only did it murder my fears, but it also murdered the cancer in the process. I became a replacement expert. When symptoms tried to rise up against me, I started using more of God's Word to replace anything that may have crept up inside of me. I started confessing God's Word on healing. I would say out loud…

O LORD my God, I cried out to You, and You healed me (Psalm 30:2).

Then I would say…

And when Jesus went out He saw a great multitude; and He was moved with compassion for them, and healed their sick (Matthew 14:14).

After that I reminded God of this word…

If you diligently heed the voice of the LORD your God and do what is right in His sight, give ear to His commandments and keep all His statutes, I will put none of the diseases on you which I have brought on the Egyptians. For I am the LORD who heals you (Exodus 15:26).

I began to see myself in the Scriptures. The words that God spoke were no longer words for the people in the Bible; they were for me. I began to believe His Word more than anything in the world. It's not that I have never been afraid; I just realize that, if I am afraid, I can attack my fears with His Word. I've got a weapon of defense against the enemy.

Knowing that the Lord is my shepherd gives me the faith not to be afraid. But not until I have a revelation and a clear understanding of the reality of God's Word will I walk in that level of faith. I can know all day long that God is *a* shepherd. That won't help me. It's not until I recognize that He is *my* shepherd that I become full of faith. I've replaced my fear with faith. Believe me when I tell you that this will work in every area of your life.

Find out the specific scriptures in the Bible that are assigned to your problem and begin to confess those words over your life and situation every day. Write me and tell me just how your fears dissipated in the presence of the Word. It's not fear that you should be most afraid of. What's really scary is being attacked by the onslaught of the enemy and not having a word for your defense.

He will not be afraid of evil tidings; his heart is steadfast, trusting in the LORD (Psalm 112:7).

Faith Is Rewarded Immediately—
The Microwave Mentality

I fully realize that we live in a microwave generation that wants everything now. However, there are some things that you are just going to have to wait for. In the realm of the spirit God wants us to develop patience because patience works a good work in the life of the believer. Patience teaches us things about life, about our character, and about whom we really are more than anything else does. In fact, without patience, true and biblical faith cannot be produced.

True, biblical faith cannot be produced without patience.

Much of what we call faith today is really not faith at all. We sow a seed today and expect an abundant harvest tomorrow. We hate to wait. Many of us have felt that there is something inherently bad about waiting. In the natural, we realize that it takes time for seeds to grow and become mature trees. When a woman becomes pregnant it will take eight to nine months to deliver a healthy baby. In the natural, we realize these truths. But in the realm of the spirit, we expect seeds to mature overnight. That is unrealistic.

Because we have allowed this mind-set to continue and infiltrate the body of Christ, we have developed a bunch of whining babies who vent, murmur, and complain if they are not immediately satisfied when they cry for milk. I believe that this is perhaps one of the main reasons people in the body of Christ have become so spiritually immature and weak. They have not been taught about the discipline of waiting. They have not been taught that the process of waiting will build their character.

We look at a generation that promotes "the now." "If you want a house, don't worry. Put no money down. Don't worry about having money in your savings account. We will get you into your house today. We will pay your closing costs and all your points. Leave it up to us." The problem with this scenario is that, if you have not been disciplined enough to save money, you are probably not going to have the discipline to pay your mortgage in a timely fashion each month. Why? It came too quickly for you. You did not learn anything in the process.

One thing I have realized in my travels, particularly in the United States, is that church folks are in some deep debt. If you got into debt because of medical illnesses or because you chose to take care of your elderly parents, then that is acceptable. Actually it is commendable. And I believe that, because of the circumstances, God will help you get out of that debt supernaturally. For most people, however, that is not the case at all. Most people get into debt because of greed.

They get into debt trying to keep up with the Joneses. They buy things that they don't need. And the things that they do need, they do not want to wait to get them. They want them now! They refuse to adhere to a strict budget. Yet these same people will sincerely give one offering (as an attempt to get God's attention) believing that God will supernaturally get them out of their indebtedness. Can God do it? Yes. Has He done it before? Of course; the children of Israel were in debt one morning and, by the next day, they were not only debt-free, but their creditors were all drowned in the sea as well. So the issue is not about whether God can do it or if He has done it before.

The real issue is about you. It's about your patience. It is all about what you are willing to do in order to get out of your present situation and into a better one. How patient will you be in order to see God's glory in your life? Face it—you did not get into your situation overnight. It took you years to become like you are. It probably will not take you as many years to get out of your situation, but it will take you some time. And the time that it takes you is good for you.

In that time you will begin to learn lessons that are valuable. You will begin to identify how you got into the mess in the first place. Your discerning will become keener while you wait for the answer to come. I sincerely believe that the answer is on the inside of you. You really don't have to look very far. It's just that you have not been as organized as you should have been. Because of that clutter, you started looking for your answers everywhere else other than within you.

James, the brother of Jesus, wrote in his epistle an alarming truth that helps to substantiate what I am saying. He knew that patience was a necessary element in developing faith that will last over a period of time. James understood *faith that takes a lickin'*. He knew that without patience you would never have the power to last when the storms arose in life. His advice is perhaps the greatest advice on the subject of patience in the Bible. Without it you wind up receiving absolutely nothing from the Lord. Read his letter and glean from his wisdom.

> *James, a bondservant of God and of the Lord Jesus Christ, to the twelve tribes which are scattered abroad: Greetings. My brethren, count it all joy when you fall into various trials, knowing that the testing of your faith produces patience. But let patience have its perfect work, that you may be perfect and complete, lacking nothing. If any of you lacks wisdom, let him ask of God, who gives to all liberally and without reproach, and it will be given to him. But let him ask in faith, with no doubting, for he who doubts is like a wave of the sea driven and tossed by the wind. For let not that man suppose that he will receive anything from the Lord; he is a double-minded man, unstable in all his ways (James 1:1-8).*

We Are Always Capable of Judging Faith in Others

All church people—no matter what denomination and affiliation they are—tend to be judgmental. It is a sad trait that too many Christians have in common. Somehow, somewhere along the line, we got this idea that we can judge if a person has faith or not. I realize that this could be a pretty touchy subject. Many people believe that God has called them to be "fruit inspectors"

148

in that they can pronounce judgments and verdicts over other believers' lives.

As merit worthy as that may sound, *no one* has the authority to cast judgment on anyone. Only God has that prerogative. Why is this important? We have to be careful in this because faith is an area that we don't always get to preview what God is doing in the lives of His children. The master sculptor or the skilled artist never unveils his or her masterpiece before the proper time of completion.

It's the same way with the people whom God is working through to develop patience and good character in also. God is working on a masterpiece in you, yet His work is in the rough. He cannot reveal His work too soon. If He did, you would not be able to understand why everything looks so displaced.

For example, imagine that your car engine needs repairing and you set up a time to take it to your favorite mechanic. Suppose you showed up at the garage while he was working on your car. You might be a little concerned if you saw your car engine in pieces all over the floor, like a giant puzzle. That's the way it looks to you, but to him it doesn't look like chaos. He sees it all as a work in progress; he sees the engine completely rebuilt and whole. In his eyes, your car is on the road and running smoothly.

God is like that mechanic. He sees us on the road and running smoothly. We may look like a mess right now, but not for long. So if you make the mistake of judging my faith based on where I am today, you will definitely miss it. You can't judge where I am going based on where I am now. The reason you shouldn't make your assessment too soon is simply because, right now, I am in God's repair shop. He has all of the certified parts to fix me properly. Best of all, I am on His schedule, not yours. He's going to release me when it's His time.

I've seen many Christians get discouraged and want to give up because their faith was judged based on where they are right now. Unfortunately, they were judged by so-called "seasoned Christians." Can you really say that a person does not have faith just because you don't see the immediate manifestation? That's totally unfair. God has some people in the making. They are in their process. Sometimes processes take time. Most processes that we go through never accurately reflect what we are going to look like in the final analysis.

I have some beautiful grandchildren. I remember when they were born. Suppose I judged what they were going to become and what their effectiveness on society would be based on how they looked and acted when they were just toddlers? That may have been a frightening thought. No, I had to wait and give them time to grow and to mature. They needed time to develop, time to make mistakes and learn from those mistakes. Their faith, too, needed to be tested from toddler years to little children years to teenager years and beyond.

In short, it is a grave misconception to believe that you have the power to limit someone's future based on where he or she is now. Get this in your spirit: You don't have the right to judge what God has created. He gave everybody a specific purpose in life. Not everybody realizes that purpose, but that's okay. Some folks may need a bit more time than others do. Some may never realize their potential. But it's still not your job to judge them. Don't judge your brothers' or sisters' faith; encourage them. Remember too that if you judge, in time you, too, will come under someone else's judgment—possibly God's.

Judge not, that you be not judged (Matthew 7:1).

The Words I Say Don't Really Amount to Much As It Relates to My Faith

You are snared by the words of your mouth; you are taken by the words of your mouth (Proverbs 6:2).

Let's look at the definition of the word *snare.*

snare
1 a (1) : a contrivance often consisting of a noose for entangling birds or mammals... **b** (1) : something by which one is entangled, involved in difficulties, or impeded (2) : something deceptively attractive **2** ... **a** : one of the catgut strings or metal spirals of a snare drum...[2]

This area is perhaps the one where most believers mess up the most. Far too many Christians falsely believe that words are harmless and don't have an effect on the quality of their life. Nothing *Your words* could be further from the truth. Your words mean everything. In fact, you *mean* and the life that you live right now *everything.* are the sum total of the words you've been speaking all of your life.

You cannot flippantly use your words to speak of sickness, sin, and poverty and expect that your words won't produce those negative results in your life. The Bible says that we are snared by our words. This verb *snared* is linked to the noun *snare* we defined above. A snare is a trap for birds and small mammals and is literally anything dangerous. Those definitions alone would compel me to be far more careful about the words that I use.

Another definition has to do with the spiraled wires strung across the bottom of a snare drum, which cause it to produce a tight, crisp sound. In other words, the snare produces a sound that it normally wouldn't produce if the wires weren't there. Could it be that your words are producing results that would be far different if you made the choice to change what you say?

You become trapped by your words just like a small animal is trapped. You can't get out unless someone comes to release you. Well, consider me that someone. "In the name of Jesus Christ of Nazareth, I release you now from the trap of your own tongue, never to be imprisoned by its careless remarks ever again." Now your tongue needs to say, "I receive it in Jesus' name."

You see, you just can't go around casually talking about how sickly you are. You can't make empty jokes about poverty or being poor. You will get what you say. Faith really does have a voice. I've known people who kept talking about how they grew up in a cursed family. Little did they realize that they were actually creating a cursed environment for their own family.

Even though the family member whom they were talking about had been dead for nearly two decades, they still talked about that person's negative traits and cursed ways as if he or she was still alive and well. In many ways that person still was alive and well since their family members gave a voice to the curses of his or her past. Remember this: Whatever you refuse to rehearse, God will eventually reverse. On the other hand, the more you rehearse negative thoughts and speak them, the more they will become your reality.

In the same way that a professional hunter lays a trap for his prey, your tongue captures you and brings your entire body, soul, and spirit into subjection to what you spoke. Like God is, you and your words become one. Just knowing that truth alone should make you far more conscious of what comes out of your mouth from this day forward.

Whatever God's Going to Do, He Is Going to Do; My Faith Won't Make Any Difference at All

I think this statement is a cop-out for many Christians. People like to put all the work on God. In other words, they don't like to believe that they should do anything to contribute to their deliverance process. Let me remind you that faith is all about action. The Acts of the Apostles in the Bible is a book full of the acts of faith that the apostle performed. They knew well that God could do anything He wanted to because He is God.

Faith is all about action.

However, God needs someone to do His work. He needs some initiators, some folks who are willing to step out of the boat and walk on the water. Peter was this kind of person. He could have stayed in the boat when he saw Jesus. There was safety in the boat. There was a comfort zone to staying in the boat. However, it didn't require any faith at all to simply stay in the boat.

I sometimes wonder—Peter being as influential as he was—where the church of the Lord Jesus Christ would be today if he had decided to stay in the boat. Suppose Peter had had the attitude, "If God wants me to walk on the water, then He'll just make it happen. If God wants me to be healed, He'll just heal me. If God wants me to be rich, He'll just send money from the sky. There's nothing that I can do to help God." What cop-out talking! The main problem with that kind of jargon is that it won't produce

154

anything in the kingdom of God. God is waiting for some-body to get the party started and destroy the works of the devil. You may say, "Well, when God moves on me to do something, I will and not until." I've got news for you. You may be waiting your whole life for that to happen, and it may never happen for you. God is moved by our acts of faith. Your faith is the only thing that really captures the attention of God. Just read the following text:

> *And when the disciples saw Him walking on the sea, they were troubled, saying, "It is a ghost!" And they cried out for fear. But immediately Jesus spoke to them, saying, "Be of good cheer! It is I; do not be afraid." And Peter answered Him and said, "Lord, if it is You, command me to come to You on the water." So He said, "Come." And when Peter had come down out of the boat, he walked on the water to go to Jesus. But when he saw that the wind was boisterous, he was afraid; and begin-ning to sink he cried out, saying, "Lord, save me!" And immediately Jesus stretched out His hand and caught him, and said to him, "O you of little faith, why did you doubt?"* (Matthew 14:26-31).

Peter was not obligated to do anything. He could have chilled out in the boat just like the others did. But he made the decision to do something that he had never done before. He did not have a "walk on the water" owner's manual. Peter never took surfing lessons. Yet, he tried. He did his best. His action of faith was what prompted the Lord to act on Peter's behalf.

My dear brother or sister, I earnestly pray that this book *Faith That Takes a Lickin'* has sparked a fire on the inside of you to do what no man or woman has ever done before. In the name of Jesus Christ, I commission you to do greater works than any person in your generation. I command you to run the most profitable businesses in the world. Make more money than any believer has ever made. Build the largest churches that the world has ever seen.

Fill those churches up with millions of members. It's never been done before, but you can do it. Purchase civic centers and convert them into sanctuaries for His glory. In the areas of the sciences, arts and humanities, do what no other person has ever dared to do before. Be a trendsetter. Don't be limited by your past. And for goodness' sake, don't be limited by the pasts of others.

God has given you an unusual ability to create wealth, to change lives, and to advance His kingdom. The choice is all yours. Will you wait on an ethereal voice to call out your name, or will you go in faith and do mighty exploits because you know God? I trust that you will use your faith to make a real difference all over the world. You've got a different kind of faith.

It's not the faith that lasts from one Sunday until the next. You've got faith that will stand after every attack of the enemy—*faith that takes a lickin'*. One of these days, when we stand before God, you just might hear God saying to me or possibly even to you, "Yes, My son, yes, My daughter, you didn't die; you didn't give up or falter. You've kept the faith. You've taken a licking and you are still ticking. Enter into the joy of the Lord."

> *I have fought the good fight, I have finished the race, I have kept the faith. Finally, there is laid up for me the crown of righteousness, which the Lord, the righteous Judge, will give to me on that Day, and not to me only but also to all who have loved His appearing* (2 Timothy 4:7-8).

> *But without faith it is impossible to please Him, for he who comes to God must believe that He is, and that He is a rewarder of those who diligently seek Him* (Hebrews 11:6).

Endnotes

1. National Prayer News Service, "How to Keep the Pastor You Love" by Krista K. Carnet. <http://hispowerportal.com/nw/index.php3?grpid=40&articleid=1318> 6 May 2005.

2. *Merriam-Webster's Collegiate Dictionary*, 10th edition (Springfield, Massachusetts: Merriam-Webster, Inc., 1996), "snare."

About the Author

Jack Coe, Jr., is the oldest child of Jack Coe, Sr., a widely known healing evangelist and tent revival preacher of the 1940's and 50's. Jack Junior also heeded God's call to become a full-time evangelist in 1986, even in the midst of a battle with colon cancer. Today, healed and whole, Jack Coe, Jr., and his wife, Frieda, conduct miracle crusades around the world and minister the Gospel message everywhere they travel.

To contact the Coes, write to:

Christian Fellowship
PO Box 398538
Dallas, TX 75339
www.jackcoe.org